Poverty Alleviation and MGNREGA

A Rights Based Policy

DR. RIMKI PATGIRI

Highbrow Scribes Publications
New Delhi

First Published 2018

ISBN : 978-81-936572-7-0

Published by
Highbrow Scribes Publications
55-C, Jhang Apartments, Sector-13
Rohini, New Delhi -110085

Mobile : +91-8826398333
+91-7982333488
E-mail : highbrowscribes@gmail.com
Website : www.highbrowscribes.com

Typeset and cover design by
Shagun Graphics, Delhi-110086

Contents

Preface

Mahatma Gandhi National Rural Employment Guarantee Act (MGNREGA) was enacted with objective for strengthening livelihood security by creating employment, ecological assets creation and rural infrastructure. The Act provides strengthening of decentralised governance in the implementation of scheme which aims to reduce poverty, distress migration and employment of women in rural areas. It has designed primarily as a social safety net and the potential to transform rural India into a more productive, equitable, connected society. Earlier, employment guarantee programmes in India were targeted at the poor and were generally identified with poverty alleviation. The MGNREGA goes beyond poverty alleviation and recognises employment as a legal right. Especially for women, MGNREGA is an important source of work and income. The Act has been designed especially to allow women equity in both access to work and in the payment of wages.

In many parts of the country, tremendous success has been noted at the community and individual level in terms of natural resource conservation and regeneration, improvement in rural connectivity, reduced wage discrimination, rural to urban migration, etc. The most significant fact of this Act is that it has given priority to the rural people to demand for work; those who are willing to do unskilled manual work for their livelihood. In the Financial Year (FY) 2018-19, total 176.82 crore person days of work has been generated in across the country. There is additional person days provided to the states and the districts according to the demands and needs of the beneficiaries. The most significant step has been taken by ministry is the convergence of MGNREGA with other schemes which has helped to create sustainable and productive assets. As per the data provided by MGNREGA website, 3.92 crore assets has been created across the country during the FY 2018-19. Further, the scheme has high expectation in terms of poverty alleviation, assets creation, income generation, etc.

MGNREGA is the only poverty alleviation scheme which gives the central place to the Gram Panchayats. This is one of the bottom-up features of the programme. As per the Act, Section 16 (1), MGNREGA works is implemented in the Gram Panchayat that ensures active participation of the Gram Sabha members. Apart from these, MGNREGA provides scope to women to participate in the process of planning and implementation of the scheme such as conducting social audit as members of Gram Sabha and Gram Panchayat. So, it is an institution of potential, it is a local government system where women have a say, more than anywhere in the world, in India. This is one of the few public programmes where the content is shaped really from the bottom, from the workers; it is worker-centric programme.

The Government of Assam has been implementing various poverty alleviation programmes to address the problems of poverty as well as for the upliftment of economic conditions of people in the rural areas, the MGNREGA is the one of those programmes that sought to alleviate poverty and gender equity by providing employment opportunities to the rural people. MGNREGA has made potential impact in order to improve the conditions of rural people in the state through creating rural infrastructure such as afforestation, water conservation, renovation of traditional water bodies, micro-irrigation, land development, road connectivity, etc. The Ministry of Rural Development has been trying to put more effort in the implementation of the MGNREGA to meet the demand for the work in flood-affected areas and income generating assets mostly linked to augmentation of irrigation potential and thus, reducing the distress migration. The present study "Poverty Alleviation and MGNREGA: A Rights Based Policy" is focused on benefits of the scheme to overcome poverty, employment status of rural household after demand of employment, role of line departments as well as local governance in Nalbari district of Assam which is situated at the plains of the Brahmaputra Valley. In view of achieving the objectives of the study, the field study was done in Nalbari district of Assam covering 7 blocks, 14 villages and 280 households. It is also focused on the role of state agencies and covered 50 implementing officials from GP level to State level.

Author

Acknowledgements

A number of people have helped me in completing this book. I, sincerely, acknowledge their cooperation and valuable advice and express my deep appreciation to all of them. The publication of the book would not have been possible without the valuable inputs in terms of knowledge, information and time from different people.

I am deeply indebted to Prof. R. Borgohain, Department of Political Science, North-Eastern Hill University, for her critical but constructive inputs and advice has greatly enriched my research work.

I benefited from various discussions, training programmes, seminars and workshops of National Institute of Rural Development and Panchayati Raj (NIRDPR), Hyderabad. It is a privilege and a great advantage to have free access to knowledge and experience.

I am grateful to the inspiration given by Dr. Ajay M. Gondane, Indian High Commissioner to Australia, Ministry of External Affairs, India.

This investigation would not have been successfully completed without the cooperation of the people of Nalbari district of Assam as well as officials from District Rural Development Agency, Development Blocks and Gram Panchayats in Nalbari district. I thank them for giving time from their busy schedules to respond to my queries.

I am extremely grateful to all my family members for their prayers, love, support, and encouragement throughout my study. My special gratitude goes to my Mom and Dad and my elder sister and brother for their endless support and dedication towards making my work a success.

This work is dedicated to my dear sister, Dreambeauti Patgiri, who left us forever on 28.01.2016.

Author

1 Background of the Study

Poverty is multi-faced and it limits a person in many ways. It is both widespread and intensive, and intrinsically related to socio-cultural, socio-political and economic factors. Amartya Sen defines poverty not only as the denial of freedom, opportunities and choices that are basic to human development[1] but also as a deprivation of basic capabilities. Poverty has been defined as a deprivation of the basic necessities of life.[2] It is understood as people's inability to fulfill their basic requirements for subsistence i.e. food, clothing and shelter which are leads to physical deprivation. It is considered as a major challenge for development planning in India as large number of its population still live below the poverty line. Poverty in India is extensive because of its high population growth rate, agrarian form of economy, primitive agricultural practices, illiteracy, ignorance, unemployment, caste-based politics, urban rural divide, social iniquity and discrimination. In addition, India has also experienced economic crisis due to alarming rise in prices of consumer goods and services as well as productive input as a result of inflation in the form of price rise of food, fertilisers, oil, metals and machinery in international economy during the initial periods after independence. In India, poverty is predominantly found in rural areas where majority of its population belong to the categories of landless labourers, agricultural labourers, marginal and small farmers, self-employed, vendors, hawkers, rural artisans, etc. Rural areas are characterised by conditions such as malnutrition, ill-heath, unsanitary conditions, illiteracy, unemployment, etc. which indicate the level of poverty in these areas. Although the records of rural poverty in terms of education, level of consumption and basic health has declined, for example, mobility in education has improved significantly across generations for all major social groups and wealth classes. However, in other dimensions, especially uneven economic growth, nutrition, women and children health, morbidity rate problems remain stubborn and are worse for the poor especially in rural areas. Rural areas are diversifying away from agriculture toward the non-farm sector. India is slowly becoming urbanised. The trend of non-farm employment has become casual and its quality is declining. Although considerable progress has been achieved through self-employment/non-farm activity in terms of household income and access to education however, inequalities are visible in the economic growth, e.g. Kerala and Tamil Nadu have nutrition and human development outcomes comparable with the developed countries but in States such as Bihar, Madhya Pradesh, Orissa, and Uttar Pradesh, the condition is bad. The infant mortality rate, morbidity rate, and child immunisation is increasing, taking a significant toll on productive capabilities in rural areas. That is why poverty has continued to fall apace, even as agricultural growth has slowed. The government has taken many initiatives to alleviate the poverty such as Sarva Shiksha Abhiyan for education, National Rural Health Mission for health, Pradhan Mantri Awas Yojana for housing, Mahatma Gandhi National Rural Employment Guarantee Act for employment and livelihood, etc.

Assam is primarily a rural state with more than 98 per cent of its area falling under rural areas and 86 per cent rural population.[3]Assam is rich in natural resources in comparison to many other states in northeast India but due to the absence of proper utilisation of such resources, it is considered as one of the least developed states in India.[4] According to 2011 Census, the population of the state is 3,11,69,272 out of which 2,67,80,516 live in the rural areas[5] and more than 50 per cent of its population is engaged in the agricultural.[6] Further, Planning Commission of India 2011-12, states that Assam is the eighth highest as far as the population living in the BPL segment is concerned.[7] Also, as far as the percentage of BPL population in Assam is concerned, it is the third highest among the eight northeastern states amongst the BPL segment in the region.[8] According to 2011-12, the poverty rate in Assam was estimated at 30 per cent (as per the official poverty line), with rural poverty being at 33.9 per cent and urban poverty at 20.5 per cent. Within Assam, several districts like Goalpara, Dhubri, Dhemaji, Morigaon, Nalbari, Kokrajhar, Darrang, and many others have poverty level much higher than that of the State of Assam as a whole.[9]

To address the problems of poverty as well as for the upliftment of economic conditions of people in the rural areas, the Government of Assam has been implementing various poverty alleviation programmes, under the Panchayat Raj Institution and Community Development Programme (CDP). Such poverty alleviation programmes were National Rural Employment Programme (NREP), Rural Landless Employment Guarantee Programme (RLEGP), Jawahar Rozgar Yojana (JRY), Integrated Rural Development Programme (IRDP), Training of Rural Youth for Self-Employment (TRYSEM), Development of Women and Children in Rural Areas (DWCRA), etc. The emphasis of the programmes was on building up of local resources by increasing the capacity of the rural poor through providing self-employment or wage employment. However, the process of implementation of such programmes was slow in Assam due to under-utilisation of funds, lack of infrastructure facilities, non-availability of inputs, lack of awareness, lack of people's participation and co-ordination among the different departments, problems in payment often less than prescribed wages and disparity between wages paid to women and men, weak monitoring and verification systems. For example, wage employment programmes were not very successful in terms of utilising the allocated resources and generating additional employment for the BPL. However, these programmes were able to create to a very limited extent, some village level assets and infrastructure in terms of schools, health centers, roads and ponds. Despite the implementation of various poverty alleviation programmes in Assam, a large number of its rural population continues to live below the poverty line. Although programmes like the SGSY and IAY were adopted to alleviate poverty in the rural areas with some special provisions for women, the rate of poverty among women continues to be high in rural areas of Assam.

According to the Planning Commission Report of 1991, Nalbari district, which is the area of the present study, had the highest number of people below poverty line in Assam.[10] The district is bounded by the Indo-Bhutan international border on northern side and on southern side by River Brahmaputra. Nalbari district consists of one civil sub-division, seven revenue circle, seven community development blocks and 456 villages. Nearly 89.28 per cent of the population of the district live in rural area and a large number of its population is dependent on agriculture. The population of Nalbari district is 7,69,919 out of which 3,95,804 and 3,74,115 are males and females respectively.[11] As per 2011 Census, the average literacy rate in the district is 89.9 per cent, out of which 93.72 per cent are males and 85.88 per cent are females. In spite of the high literacy rate in Nalbari district, the level of unemployment continues to be high. As per the Census of India, the population of Nalbari district has increased during the last 50 years. The 2011 Census shows that there was an increase of 11.99 per cent in the population compared to population as per 2001 Census.

Table 1.1: Block-wise Population of District Nalbari according to 2011 Census.

Sl. No.	Blocks	Male	Female	Total
1.	Pub-Nalbari	65,410	61,577	1,26,987
2.	Borigog Banbhag	54,106	51,695	1,05,801
3.	Paschim Nalbari	60,541	57,869	1,18,410
4.	Madhupur	25,770	24,078	49,848
5.	Tihu	39,099	37,600	76,699
6.	Barbhag	30,593	29,114	59,707
7.	Barkhetri	1,03,949	98,247	2,02,196

Source: nalbari.nic.in/census

Agriculture of crops like paddy, jute, sugarcane, pulses, and mustard is the main occupation among the rural people. Further, Nalbari district is considered backward in terms of infrastructure, rural connectivity due to absence of entrepreneurship, capital investment and marketing of products. Poverty, unemployment and landlessness are some of the major problems faced by people here. There are no large industries in the district. It is also one of the flood-affected districts of Assam. Further, the human resources of the district have not been fully utilised due to the lack of proper planning and systematic approach. According to the Assam Human Development Report 2014, the poverty rate in the district is 33 per cent. Because of these reasons, huge number of people have migrated to the urban areas from rural areas.[12] There are different types of land available in Nalbari which could be utilised to generate sources of revenue for the district. (See Table1.2).

Table 1.2: Land Use Pattern in District Nalbari, 2010-2011.

Sl. No.	Used Land	Area in hectares
1.	Total Geographical area	1,00,483
2.	Land not available for cultivation	26,325
3.	Land put to non-agricultural uses	19,925
4.	Barren and un-cultural land	6,400
5.	Other non-cultivated land excluding fallow land	3,027
6.	Permanent pastures and other grazing land	1,338
7.	Land under trees, groves, etc. not included in net area	582
8.	Cultivable waste land	1,907
9.	Fallow land	3,401
10.	Fallow other than current fallow	3,302
11.	Current fallow	99
12.	Net area sown	67,730
13.	Total cropped area	1,13,916
14.	Area sown more than one	46,186

Source: Statistical Hand-book Assam, 2012.

Many of the earlier government schemes and programmes for rural development and poverty alleviation which had been undertaken are reported to have failed to achieve the desired objectives in the state, in general and Nalbari district, in particular. The state agencies also could not implement these programmes effectively due to heavy pressure from various quarters like political leaders and other vested interests.

Given this socio-economic context, MGNREGA was seen as a positive solution to these problems, which sought to alleviate poverty and gender equity by providing employment opportunities to the rural people. The study has examined whether MGNREGA has been able to alleviate poverty, in general and of women, in particular in Nalbari district of Assam, by undertaking a critical study of the programme, its implementation and the role of various implementing agencies, NGOs, political parties, etc.

Review of Literature

A number of studies have been done on various aspects of poverty by various scholars and academics. Following are some of the studies based on poverty, poverty alleviation programmes, women and poverty, and MGNREGA.

Conceptual Review

Amartya Sen's, *Poverty and Famine: An Essay on Entitlement and Deprivation,* mainly focusses on the causation of starvation in general and famines in particular. He has taken a brief account of the concept and approaches of poverty. He has explained the problems of conceptualisation and measurement of poverty. He has illustrated some of the case studies of famine situation from different parts of the world i.e. *the Great Bengal Famine of 1943, the Ethiopia Famines of 1973-75, Famines in the Sahel regions of Africa during the early 1970s and the Bangladesh Famines of 1974.* Different approaches have been used (biological inadequacy, the inequality and relative deprivation) for conceptualising and defining poverty. Lastly, he looks at general issues of deprivation related to entitlement system.[13]

Poverty in India, by V.M. Dandekar and Nilakanth Rath, was the first systematic work in the country to determine poverty. This study was concerned with the problems of poverty in India with particular references to rural India. In their view, the problem of low income, unequal distribution of resources and slow pace of development is a great threat in rural India. They also observed that small gain in policy formulation and its implementation in the rural areas are another causes of poverty which needed urgent attention.[14]

P. Sainath, in his book *Everybody Loves a Good Drought: Stories from Indian Poorest Districts,* is a well-organised work related to poverty and hunger victim people of Bihar, Tamil Nadu, Madhya Pradesh and Orissa. The author has highlighted some of the poorest districts in southern parts of Orissa. He has explained the poverty scenario of Malkangiri, Koraput, Kalahandi, Bolangir and Nuapada districts. He has mainly highlighted the suffering of the marginalised people of the four states and made the concerned people aware and forced them to think about these issues.[15]

Keshav Dev Gaur, in his book *Poverty Alleviation and Rural Diversification* focusses on the various anti-poverty programmes (especially IRDP) and the multi-dimensional nature of poverty. This scholar has explained the extent of poverty in India with particular reference to Rajasthan. According to him, poverty is the most important problem which directly impact Indian economy. The author explained in detail about the Integrated Rural Development Programme's aims and objectives. He also observed that Integrated Rural Development Programme has played an important role in alleviating poverty in India. Lastly, the author has found that lack of sources of irrigation, big size of family, more dependence on the head of households, absence of the other sources of economic activities, joint family system, and unemployment were the major contributory factors for existence of poverty in the study area.[16]

Rudra P. Pradhan in his article, "An Economic Approach between Human Development and Poverty in northeast region of India," is based on field study of poverty affected districts of northeast region in India. In this article, he tries to relate the human development and poverty issue in this region. He observed that the extent of income poverty is very close to social poverty because it shows that where social poverty is high, income poverty is also high. He has examined that the level of human development is high in Mizoram, Manipur, and Nagaland and in Arunachal Pradesh, Assam, Meghalaya and Tripura is low. On the other hand, the rate of poverty is low in Mizoram, Manipur, Nagaland, Sikkim and Arunachal Pradesh, Assam, Meghalaya and Tripura is high. Finally, he proved that human development has a significant role to alleviate poverty in the northeast India.[17]

Policy-Based Review

Joyeeta Ahmed, in her book *Poverty Alleviation in Assam,* explains about the natural resources of Assam and economic problems of the state. The author discussed about the economic backwardness of the state which forces its people to a life of distress and poverty. Further, she explains that the regional imbalance, absence of adequate infrastructure, flood, soil erosion and occasional drought are the main causes of poverty. She emphasised that unemployment is the main crux behind the problem of poverty in the state. She also explained that various poverty alleviation programmes have been implemented like, TRYSEM, DWCRA, NREP, RLEGP and FWP, but there has not been applicable improvement in poverty situation of the state.[18]

Pinaki Chakraborty's article "Implementation of Employment Guarantee: A Preliminary Appraisal," is based on the state-wise employment demand-supply data and the use of funds released under the National Rural Employment Guarantee Act by the central government. The author examines the budgetary incidence and spatial dimension of the progress of implementation of the Act across the states in India. The data used in this article does not cover the entire year but is based on the monthly data of the first few months provided on the progress of implementation of the National Rural Employment Guarantee Act. It highlights the implementation of MGNREGA by discussing more details about the agencies involved and funding pattern. This article discussed about the implementation of MGNREGA in 200 districts in the first phase. Finally, the author suggests that the performance of MGNREGA implementation need to be developed with suitable indicators which would reflect the demand side or the preference for the MGNREGA among the rural households and also the supply side performance or the performance of the government.[19]

K.R.Venugopal in his article, "The Reluctant Guarantee", traces a comparative account of the Employment Assurance Scheme (EAS) and National Rural Employment Guarantee Act (NREGA). The author treats NREGA as a mode of raising our voices on behalf of the poor to expand their rights. He says rural unemployment is the crux of the problem of poverty. He also explained in detail about the NREGA aims and objectives. He draws some shortfalls in this programme and suggests some modifications. He said that all the crucial provisions in NREGA 2005 undermines the proclaimed guarantee and it would be idle to pretend that this Act would 'change the geography of poverty', in its present form. Finally, he suggests that all the poor-unfriendly provisions in the NREGA need to be removed or changed on the suggested lines to defend and expand the rights of the poor and provide them with an employment guarantee that truly promotes a genuine right to work for the rural poor.[20]

Bela Bhatia and Jean Dreze in their article "Employment Guarantee in Jharkhand: Ground Realities," discuss various aspects of the implementation of National Rural Employment Guarantee Act in the light of the field investigation. This article is based primarily on first-hand observation from the field survey of two remote and deprived blocks (i.e. Palamu and Latehar) of Jharkhand State. The authors mentioned a few implementation problems of NREGA in the survey areas. They found that due to low awareness among the people of those areas, the NREGA programme is not implemented with the proper guidelines. In Jharkhand, there are no Gram Panchayats since 1978, and so the entire programme implementation work has been assigned to the Gram Sabha. It has also shown in the study areas that there is a crucial gap between the Programme Officer at the Block Level, Gram Rozgar Sevaks at the Panchayat Level, Supervisors and the Engineers. Lastly, the authors concluded by comparing the NREGA implementation in the two States i.e. Jharkhand and Rajasthan.[21]

"Work fare as an Effective Way to Fight Poverty: A Case of India's NREGS", by Shamika Ravi and Monika Engler analyses the impact of MGNREGA on the rural poor households. The study discusses about the impact of the programme on food security, savings and health. The authors mention that the performance of MGNREGA is high in Andhra Pradesh as compared to other states. The research indicates that MGNREGA significantly increases monthly per capita expenditure on food and non-food items. It helps to improve food security by reducing the number of meals foregone. Further, they observe that the people's participation in MGNREGA increases the probability of savings by households.[22]

Jogender Sharma in his article "Potential and Challenges" proposed the potential and challenges for National Rural Employment Guarantee Act, pointed out that NREGA has the potential to transform rural economy especially for landless and the marginal farmers. The author also mentioned a few implementation problems of NREGA i.e. the programme has not focussed on minimum quality of assets that are sought to be created through this scheme. Further, the author concluded the possibility to bridge the gap between what the rural people expecting from the scheme and what the government was focussing to achieve challenges.[23]

Vijay Kumar in his article "Mahatma Gandhi National Rural Employment Guarantee Act – A Review," discussed about the salient features of MGNREGA and the various findings that were achieved after the implementation of the scheme. The author has pointed out that the share of women in work force has increased rapidly and also benefitted them. Further, the author criticised some of the shortcomings of the scheme i.e. low wages are paid than that stipulated by the Act in some states and also funds are not being appropriately utilised in some other states.[24]

K. Pattanaik's article "National Rural Employment Guarantee Scheme: Some Preliminary findings from Hoshiarpur District," highlighted that NREGS has been success in achieving equity, while its efficiency is still a question to be effectively dealt by the implementing officials of the programme. He said that women beneficiaries were benefitted through NREGS in some areas in terms of increasing their strength to fulfill their needs such as clothes for their children, expenditure on the education of the children, etc. The author concluded that the implementation of NREGS in the sub-mountainous part of the Hoshiarpur district would not raise the livelihood of the people.[25]

Abusaleh Shariff's article "Assessment of Outreach and Benefits of National Rural Employment Guarantee Scheme of India," is based on official, statistical and survey data from seven northern states with reference to the assessment of outreach and benefits of MGNREGA scheme in India. The author pointed out that NREGA has the potential to address both sustenance of income and enhance the social welfare of households in the rural areas. Further, the author said that for the effective implementation of the scheme or to overcome from negative factors was needed for effective review of the scheme.[26]

P.C. Sikligar in his article "Impact Assessment of Wage Employment (MGNREGS): A Study in Tripura," made an attempt to understand the implementation and monitoring mechanism of the scheme at grass root level as well as implications of the scheme. The author tries to explore the various entitlements of the scheme such as level of awareness, process of getting job card, etc. The author stated that majority of respondents were not aware about the Right to Information Act which is included under the scheme. Further, the author suggested that raising the efficiency in mode of payment and increase of payment of wages will strengthen the effort to achieve the objectives of the scheme.[27]

Yanyan Liu and Christopher B. Barrett in their article "Heterogeneous Pro-Poor Targeting in India's Mahatma Gandhi National Rural Employment Guarantee Scheme," traces the pro-poor as well as self-targeting features of MGNREGA. The authors' analyse the data on the basis of 66th round of the National Sample Survey conducted from July 2009 to June 2010. They emphasise that the administrative rationing of MGNREGA jobs is not pro-poor but rather exhibits a sort of middle-class bias. Further, the authors mention that the implementation problems amongst the state agencies lead to poor implementation of MGNREGA. Lastly, they explained that the level of participation is very low in Assam, Bihar, Gujarat, Haryana, Jharkhand, Karnataka, Kerala, Maharashtra, Odisha, Punjab and Uttar Pradesh.[28]

K.B. Nidheesh's article "National Rural Employment Guarantee Programmes and Amelioration of Poverty among Tribal People,"made an attempt to study the basic objective features as well as implementation of the scheme. The author pointed out that MGNREGA has benefitted the tribal people in terms of fulfilling their basic amenities which are needed for their daily life.[29]

Aruna Kanchi in her article "Can an employment guarantee scheme guarantee livelihood and food security," highlighted the Maharashtra employment scheme, with specific focus on gendered impact on livelihood and food security. She says female participation in MEGS has been high. Because the large percentage of women in MEGS is the extension of pre-dominance in agriculture, particularly among casual agricultural labour and there is limited scope for diversification of work opportunity with in rural areas and outside for women. Finally, she gave two suggestions to make the scheme more beneficial to women. First, NREGS site could be made a focal point for mobilising as well as for the delivery of social services, which could be taken advantage for raising consciousness of women to make them aware of the provisions of scheme. She says that to avoid the indefinite perpetuation of the scheme based on unskilled employment, strategies to impart skill training particularly to female participants.[30]

Ashok Pankaj and Rukmini Tankha in their article, "Empowerment Effects of the NREGS on Women Workers: A Study in Four States," made an attempt to examine the role of MGNREGA on women empowerment at both the individual and community levels. The authors analysed some of the positive impacts of MGNREGA through which women beneficiaries were benefitted because of paid employment, which has effect on intra-household, income consumption, community level as well as enhancing their choice and capabilities. Further, the author criticised that due to absence of worksite facilities and presence of contractors at the worksite, the programme failed to achieve desired objectives.[31]

Rituparna Bhattacharyya and Polly Vauquline in their article, "A Mirage or a Rural Life Line?, Analysing the impact of Mahatma Gandhi Rural Employment Guarantee Act on Women Beneficiaries of Assam," discussed from feminist perspective on gender, poverty and women empowerment and MGNREGA. The authors pointed out that women were confronted with various problems and challenges under MGNREGA such as exploitation in worksite, patriarchal norms and values, lack of worksite facilities, etc. Further, the authors pointed out that although MGNREGA has a connection between gender equality and poverty alleviation, however, persistence of gender inequality results in a chain of exploitation and vulnerability of women.[32]

Identified Research Gap

Review of literature shows that several studies and surveys have been undertaken with regard to poverty and implementation of various poverty alleviation programmes including MGNREGA in different parts of the country. However, not much work has been done on poverty and poverty alleviation in Assam. It is rare to find out about implementation of MGNREGA in Assam and almost negligible for Nalbari district. Therefore, the present study is an attempt at filling this gap.

Objectives of the Study

The main objective of the study is to examine, analyse and assess:

- the working of MGNREGA in Nalbari district of Assam;
- the role of Gram Panchyats, Programme Officer, DRDA, BDOs, political parties, NGOs in the implementation of the MGNREGA;

- the extent to which MGNREGA has been able to alleviate poverty, in general, and of women, in particular, in Nalbari district of Assam.

Methodology for the Study

The study is descriptive and analytical in nature. The data for the study was collected from both primary and secondary sources. Primary data was collected from the beneficiaries with the help of both structured and unstructured questionnaires and interviews with beneficiaries, officials from sectoral departments/line departments and elected representatives of PRIs of the study area. The study has covered all the seven community development blocks of Nalbari district of Assam. The main focusses of the study are whether rural people are getting work under MGNREGA after demand of employment like:

- Percentage women participation.
- Available facilities provided for women beneficiaries.
- Extent of income generated by the household under MGNREGA.
- Role of line departments for the implementation of MGNREGA.
- Role of Gram Panchayats to generate awareness amongst beneficiaries and the implementation process.

Sampling Framework

A sample of 280 respondents was drawn for the purpose of the study through stratified random sampling. Multi-stage random sampling method was used to collect data for the study. At the first stage, one panchayat from each block was selected through random sampling method and again from each panchayat, two villages were drawn through simple random sampling. From each village, a sample of 20 (10 male and 10 female) beneficiaries was selected from the list of beneficiaries through stratified random sampling to examine the implementation of the MGNREGA for poverty alleviation.

The second group of sample was drawn through purposive sampling from implementing officials of MGNREGA. This group includes Block Development Officers from each block, officials from sectoral departments, members of Gram Panchayat from each panchayat and NGOs.

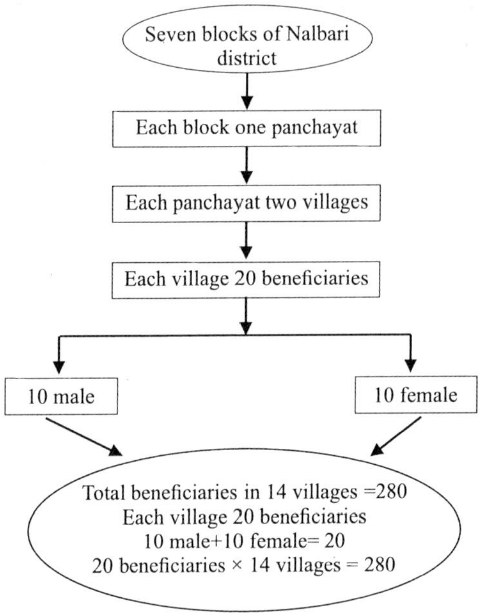

Fig. 1.1: Stages of Sampling

Primary data was collected from various field study reports and documents of DRDA (Nalbari), reports of the Ministry of Rural Development, Ministry of Law and Justice, Planning Commission Report, Census (New Delhi), etc. State government reports include report of Directorate of Economics and Statistics, Annual Reports (Assam) and Director of Rural Development and Panchayati Raj (Assam).

Secondary data was collected from existing literature like books, articles, journals and newspapers relevant to this study. Data collected from both primary and secondary sources were quantified using SPSS and simple statistical methods like percentage and average and the data was analysed in qualitative terms.

Chapter Design

The study is divided into seven chapters. The findings based on this analysis are presented in the remaining chapters. Second chapter discusses conceptual framework of poverty and poverty alleviation. Third chapter critiques various poverty alleviation programmes introduced by the Government of India. Further, fourth chapter includes a thorough discussion of the provisions and objectives of MGNREGA and its implementation. The role of state agencies and political parties in the implementation of MGNREGA is examined in chapter five. Chapter six examines whether MGNREGA has been able to alleviate poverty in general and women in particular in Nalbari district. In the chapter seven, findings and observation of the study are summarised.

References

1. Amartya Sen, *Poverty and Famines: An Essay on Entitlement and Deprivation,* Delhi: Oxford University Press, 1981.
2. Robert Chambers, "What is Poverty? Who Asks? Who Answers?", in UNDP International. Poverty Center (ed.), *Poverty in Focus*, Brazil: UNDP, 2006, pp. 3-4.
3. Government of Assam, *Economic Survey of Assam, 2012-13*, Directorate of Economic and Statistics, Planning and Development Department, 2013.
4. Government of Assam, *Economic Survey of Assam, 2011-12,* Directorate of Economic and Statistics, Planning and Development Department, 2012.
5. planningcommission.nic.in/plans/stateplan/sdr_assam/sdr_assch4.doc, accessed on May 8, 2011.
6. www.assamtribune.com, accessed on July 27, 2013.
7. planningcommission.nic.in/plans/stateplan/assam/sp_sdrassam.htm, accessed on August 12, 2012.
8. Government of Assam, Assam Human Development Report 2003, Planning and Development Department, 2013.
9. http://nalbari.nic.in, accessed on February 24, 2012.
10. Government of Assam, Assam Human Development Report 2003, Planning and Development Department, 2013.
11. http://nalbari.nic.in, accessed on September 10, 2012.
12. Government of Assam, *Economic Survey of Assam, 2011-12*, Directorate of Economics and Statistics, 2012.
13. Amartya Sen, *Poverty and Famines: An Essay on Entitlement and Deprivation*, Delhi: Oxford University Press, 1981.
14. V. M. Dandekar and Nilakantha Rath, *Poverty in India,* Pune: Indian School of Political Economy, 1971.

15. P. Sainath, *Everybody Loves a Good Drought: Stories from Indian poorest Districts,* New Delhi: Penguin Books, 1996.
16. Keshav Dev Gaur, *Poverty Alleviation and Rural Diversification,* New Delhi: Sunrise Publications, 2007.
17. Rudra P. Pradhan, "An Economic Approach between Human Development and Poverty in North-East Region India", Information Management and Business Review, Vol.2, No.1, 2011.
18. Joyeeta Ahmed, *Poverty Alleviation in Assam*, New Delhi: Hope India Publications, 2011.
19. P. Chakraborty, "Implementation of Employment Guarantee: A Preliminary Appraisal", Economic and Political Weekly, February 2007, pp. 548-551.
20. K.R.Venugopal, "The Reluctant Guarantee", Social Change, Vol. 37, No.1, March 2007.
21. B. Bhatia and J. Dreze, "Employment Guarantee in Jharkhand: Ground Realities", Economic and Political Weekly, July 2006, pp. 3198-3202.
22. Shamika Ravi and Monika Engler, "Work Fare as an Effective Way to Fight Poverty: A Case of India's NREGS", World Development, 2013.
23. Jogender Sharma, "Potential and Challenges", Kurukshetra, Vol. 58, No. 2, December 2009, pp. 3-7.
24. Vijay Kumar S, "Mahatma Gandhi National Rural Employment Guarantee Act – A Review", Kurukshetra, Vol.59, No.3, January 2011, pp. 10-14.
25. B. K. Pattanaik, "National Rural Employment Guarantee Scheme: Some Preliminary finds from Hoshiarpur District", Kurukshetra, Vol. 57, No. 6, April 2009, pp. 35-38.
26. Abusaleh Shariff, "Assessment of Outreach and Benefits of National Rural Employment Guarantee Scheme of India", the Indian Journal of Labour Economics, Vol. 52, No.2, 2009, pp. 243-248.
27. P. C. Sikligar, "Impact Assessment of Wage Employment (MGNREGS):A Study in Tripura", Indian Journal of Public Administration, Vol. LVIII, No.1, January-March, 2012, pp. 91-95.

28. Yanyan Liu, and Christopher B. Barrett, "Heterogeneous Pro-Poor Targeting in India's Mahatma Gandhi National Rural Employment Guarantee Scheme", IFPRI Discussion Paper, International Food Policy Research Institute, 2012.
29. K. B. Nidheesh, "National Rural Employment Guarantee Programmes and Amelioration of Poverty among Tribal People", Indian Journal for Social Development, Vol.8, No.2 December 2008, pp.229-244.
30. Aruna Kanchi, "Can an Employment Guarantee Scheme Guarantee Livelihood and Food Security", in Maithreyi Krishnaraj (ed.), Gender, Food Security and Rural Livelihoods, Kolkatta: Stree Publication, 2007.
31. Ashok Pankaj, Rukmini Tankha, "Empowerment Effects of the NREGS on Women Workers: A Study in Four States", Economic and Political weekly, Vol. XLV, No.30, July 24, 2010, pp. 45-49.
32. Rituparna Bhattacharyya and Polly Vauquline, "A Mirage or a Rural Life Line?, Analysing the Impact of Mahatma Gandhi Rural Employment Guarantee Act on Women Beneficiaries of Assam", Space and Culture, Vol.1, No.1, 2013.

2 Poverty and Poverty Alleviation: A Conceptual Framework

Robert Chambers emphasised that poverty is an integrated and interlinked concept involving clusters of disadvantages, which contributes to deprivation trap and has identified these disadvantages as poor households, vulnerable households and powerless households. He argues that poverty by itself contributes to whole range of other aspects of deprivation i.e. physical weakness, vulnerability, powerlessness and isolation.[1] Physical weakness contributes to poverty through inability to engage in income-generating activities and lack of opportunities. Vulnerability leads to their exploitation because of lack of assets for livelihood. Further, powerlessness contributes to poverty as the lack of it severely limits or prevents people's access to basic resources and contributes to their isolation in the area of access to education, social services and remoteness.[2]

In economics, poverty is studied in terms of income, productive assets and living standards.[3] Some of the causes of poverty mentioned by economists include unavailability of adequate employment opportunities due to adoption of faulty economic policy, lack of investments in agriculture, slow and defective industrialisation and unequal distribution of wealth. They point out that people face difficulties in earning sufficient income to be able to mobilise the required resources to fulfill their basic needs and ensure a sustainable livelihood for them. In today's context, however, poverty has been identified not merely with unemployment but also with inequality, prevailing social norms and customs, which include lack of access to education and other basic services to sections of the society. Therefore, poverty is not seen merely as an economic problem but also as a social problem. It is said to be the cause of increased morbidity and high mortality, homelessness, social discrimination and exclusion amongst people in the society.[4]

In addition, inadequate governance, lack of opportunities, inappropriate and poor implementation of public policies and programmes, lack of access to entitlements also perpetuates poverty and creates discrimination in ownership of assets, resources and political power. In short, it is perpetuation of poverty over generations which in sociological literature, has been identified as culture of poverty. According to Amartya Sen, poverty is a complex, multifaceted term that requires a clear analysis in all dimensions. Further, he argues that the capability approach ensures the measurement of poverty rather than inadequate income as the sole variable for determination of poverty. In short, it can be said that people's well-being depend on their capabilities.[5] Further, the Human Rights Commission Report defines poverty as a situation in which there is lack of essential facilities, resulting from inadequate income. There is a socially accepted minimum level of living in every society, those who live below this level are said to live in poverty. It is defined as the failure to meet the basic human needs. The basic human needs include not only food, clothing and dwelling but also health and education. It has been pointed out that poverty means lack of opportunities/capabilities to participate in economic and political life.[6] Therefore, poverty is also seen as a political issue where power and interest groups have significant influence on patterns of distribution and the existence of poverty.[7] It leads to lack of basic capacity to participate effectively in society and in decision-making processes of civil, social, cultural and political life.[8] It also leads to lack of access to information and knowledge, lack of public awareness, limited access to political power, representation, etc. Policy formulation for poverty alleviation has been carried out within the framework of political system at the national level and relies for implementation on the state government and its machinery, the local leaders and ultimately, on the co-operation of the people. Politics seems evident as far as implementation is concerned, in the identification of beneficiaries, approval of projects and funding.[9] In most of the developing countries, the solutions for solving the rural problems depend on how country's leadership uses the state machinery to affect living conditions of the rural poor.[10]

We see that poverty has been defined in terms of chronic shortage of economic, social and political opportunities/capabilities and participation, preventing access to the benefits of economic and social development and relegating individuals to exclusion as social beings.[11] Poverty is also defined and studied as deprivation; absolute deprivation in terms of capabilities and relative deprivation in terms of income. The assets of deprivation is multi-dimensional such as a lack of specific household assets, land ownership, proper housing, and housing amenities like electricity, drinking water, toilet, etc.

Absolute and Relative Poverty

Advocates of absolute poverty[12] hold that poverty is the absence or denial of the basic economic needs for individuals in the society. It is related to human existence in physical sense of just being alive. According to World Bank, poverty and inequality is not synonymous. Poverty is said to be, on the one hand, absolute standard of living of a part of society i.e. basic necessities of life, whereas, on the other hand, inequality refers to the relative standard of living of a whole society.[13]

Absolute poverty has been defined as a situation when people do not have enough money to mobilize the required resources to fulfill their basic needs; minimum amount of goods and services for their survival i.e. food, shelter, clothing, safe drinking water, sanitation, health and education. Drewnowski and Scott defines absolute poverty as a deprivation of basic physical requirements i.e. nutrition measured by factors like intake of calories and proteins; shelter measured by the quality of dwelling; health measured by the rate of infant mortality and the availability of medical facilities and cultural needs measured by the level of education, security, leisure and recreation.[14] However, this approach has been criticised on the ground that people in different strata in society cannot be expected to have the same level of basic minimum requirements.[15]

Relative poverty[16] reflects a situation when people are poor compared to others around them, but may still have enough money to survive. It is based on cultural environment around them, not on a basic amount necessary for all humans to survive. Relative poverty changes more often and adjusts to the changes in society (food and housing becoming more expensive in certain areas, more jobs, etc.). Relative poverty is concerned with the relative position of income groups[17] to each other. Relative poverty is not understood by isolating poor and treating them as a special group. Society is seen as a series of income layers and poverty is concerned with how the bottom layers relate to the rest of the society. It is said to be a phenomenon purely due to income inequality that is present in the society.

Feminisation of Poverty

A comparative study of poverty worldwide shows that women experience poverty disproportionately as compared to men. The term, 'feminisation of poverty', coined in the 1970s by Diana Pearce, refers to the concentration of poverty among women, particularly, the female-headed households.[18] The phenomenon of feminised poverty is said to extend beyond the economic domain of income and material needs to the core of individual and family life.[19]

Definitions and measurements of women's poverty are based on the conventional measures of household income and consumption or on qualitative and quantitative measures of entitlements and capabilities.[20] It is indicated by social factors such as literacy, life expectancy, primary and secondary school enrolments, access to health care, maternal mortality rates, access to land or employment, wage differentials, average age at first marriage, fertility rates and the sex ratio. These factors are consistent with the Women in Development (WID)/Gender and Development (GAD) framework which sought to elucidate the social, economic and political positions of women. It is in the context of these social indicators, along with conventional definitions and measurements of household income and consumption that poverty among women needs to be examined.

Women poverty combines with two phenomena i.e. poverty and gender inequalities. A study on the South Asian region by Poona Wignaraja defines women poverty in three inter-related aspects. Firstly, it highlights the economic sector where women face double burden such as being a women and a poor. It is well established that poor women have the least access to basic needs i.e., food, health and education and their work remains invisible resulting from limited social recognition. Secondly, in the development process, women are still excluded from access to the benefits of growth oriented process.

Thirdly, though women play an important role in the agricultural sector where the benefits of progress have not spread in an equitable manner.[21] Further, Naila Kabeer has opined that women's poverty is determined by women's unequal role in the labour market and in spite of high participation of women in the labour market; they get low wages as well as less employment opportunities in the informal sector.[22]

A number of scholars have initially discussed about women poverty in two different ways viz. female-headed household and structural changes in economy. It is considered that poverty amongst women exists because of significant changes in the family structure in such a way that households headed by female are impacted much more by factors contributing to poverty when compared to male-headed household. On the other hand, structural changes in the economy are also contributing towards women poverty. It has resulted in the displacement of women into occupational sectors that are gender-specific, low-wage and low-benefit employment opportunities. Moreover, in knowledge-based economy, women are getting less employment opportunities as they are considered to be lacking in desired skill and education for the job.[23] Studies from both developed and developing countries show that women are more vulnerable to poverty as compared to men. In India too, the incidence of poverty amongst women is substantially higher in both rural and urban areas.

From the above, it can be noted that women are subjected more to poverty in comparison to men as they have lack of access to education, engaged in either exploitative and dangerous jobs or low paid and unpaid non-economic activities, high rate of maternal mortality, inadequate allowances, etc. and these vulnerabilities amongst women compound poverty. It, thus, deserves special attention from policy-makers in determining poverty alleviation measures and allocation of resources on the basis of gender equity.

The nature and manifestation of poverty varies from society to society and context to context. Mass poverty[24] exists in many developing countries, whereas poverty in the developed countries is said to be characterised by pockets of poverty.[25] South Asia has the world's largest agglomeration of people living in chronic poverty.

In India, substantive number of its population is said to be living below the poverty line.[26] According to various government reports, the level of poverty is highest among the historically marginalised social groups such as Scheduled Castes (SCs), Scheduled Tribes (STs), the elderly, women and the disabled. Fan Shenggen, Hazell Peter and Sukhadeo Thorat opined that the percentage of the rural population living below the poverty line has fluctuated from 50 per cent to 65 per cent prior to the mid-1960s.[27] Various economic studies have also reviewed that although rural poverty in India has constantly declined from 55 per cent to 35 per cent during 1970s to 1980s. However, various studies reveal that rural poverty is still prevalent in India. Therefore, a significant gain in rural poverty alleviation in developing countries is necessary to reach the international poverty reduction target.

In India, there are several contentious issues about the official estimate of poverty; one is related to the inclusion of minimum expenditure or consumption. The consumption basket of poor based on poverty line is derived from National Sample Survey (NSS) data of 1973-1974.[28] However, the poverty estimates by Planning Commission of India is based on Tendulkar Committee which includes health and education besides the calorie intake. The Table 2.1 below shows the percentage of population below poverty line in India.

Table 2.1: Percentage of Population below Poverty Line in India (Tendulkar Methodology).

Sl. No.	Financial Year	Rural (%)	Urban (%)	Total (%)
1.	1993-1994	51.1	31.8	45.3
2.	2004-2005	41.8	25.7	37.2
3.	2009-2010	33.8	20.9	29.8
4.	2011-2012	25.7	13.7	21.9
5.	Annual average decline: 1993-1994 to 2004-05 (percentage points per annum)	0.75	0.55	0.74
6.	Annual average decline: 2004-2005 to 2011-2012 (percentage points per annum)	2.32	1.69	2.18
7.	Annual average decline: 1993-1994 to 2011-2012 (percentage points per annum)	1.36	1.01	1.30

Source: Planning Commission (2004-05), Planning Commission (2011-12).

Data from Table 2.1 revealed that although the level of poverty in India has declined over the period, however, poverty ratio in the rural areas was high as compared to urban areas. According to the Planning Commission of India, poverty has declined from 37.2 per cent to 29.8 per cent in the period of 2004-2005 to 2009-2010,[29] which means that the level of poverty has declined by 7.3 per cent over five years. Besides, World Bank Report 2011 states that 32.7 per cent of total people of India fall below the international poverty line of US $1.25 per day.[30] The Economic Survey of India 2010-2011 quoting the Tendulkar Committee Report indicated that the poverty level is much higher than what is shown by the planning commission for the period of 1993-1994 and 2004-2005.[31]

Poverty Alleviation

Poverty alleviation describes strategies to eradicate poverty.[32] Traditionally, approach to poverty alleviation is focussed on creating systems for delivering goods and services to poor households on one hand and providing livelihood opportunities on the other.[33] It is a process which seeks to reduce the level of poverty in a community and amongst a group of people with an ultimate end of completely eradicating poverty. It is also aimed at providing greater opportunity for the poor to participate in the growth process by focussing on specific growth, which offers such opportunities.[34] Further, the growth-oriented approach has been reinforced by focussing on specific sectors which provide greater opportunities to the people to participate in the growth process. Also, poverty alleviation has been strengthened and restructured with special programmes for the weaker sections of society. Poverty alleviation efforts are also aimed at removing social and legal barriers to income growth among the poor. Poverty alleviation, therefore, becomes an important issue in the development of rural areas especially in developing countries including India.

In India, poverty alleviation has been projected as a major objective of Planning Commission since 1951. The motto of the Five Year Plan has been to alleviate age-old poverty, malnutrition, hunger, inequality and low quality of life. During the Fourth Five Year Plan period (1969-74), approach to planning was modified and special attention was paid to alleviation of poverty as well as to strengthen rural infrastructure.[35] Further, the end of Nehruvian era showed a new beginning in the field of rural development in India by shifting of strategy towards both economic growth and social justice, but in reality it failed to fulfill its promises.[36] Besides income and consumption poverty, the people are deprived in other dimensions. Poverty alleviation, therefore, continued to receive focussed attention. For the purpose of this study, poverty is being studied in the framework of absolute poverty, examining the various poverty alleviation programmes undertaken by Government of India and the implementation and performance of MGNREGA.

References

1. Robert Chambers, *Rural Development, Putting the Last First*, London: Longman Publications, 1983, pp.108-139.
2. Robert Chambers, "Whose Reality Counts?" *Environment and Urbanization*, Vol. 7, No. 1, 1995, pp. 174-175.
3. H. W. Watts, "An Economic Definition of Poverty", in D.P. Moynihan (ed.), *On Understanding Poverty*, New York: Basic Books, 1968; Michael R. Carter and Christopher B. Barrett, "The Economics of Poverty Traps and Persistent Poverty: An Asset-Based Approach", *The Journal of Rural Development Studies*, Vol. 42, No. 2, 2006, pp.178-199.
4. Yogesh Atal, *The Poverty Question: Search for Solution*, New Delhi: Rawat Publications, 2002, p.156.
5. Amartya Sen, *Development as Freedom*, New York: Oxford University Press, 1999, pp.87-90.
6. Else Oyen, S.M. Miller and Sayed Abdus Samad, *Poverty a Global Review, Handbook on International Poverty Research*, New Delhi: Rawat Publications, 2003, p.24.
7. Atal, n.4.
8. Toruquist Olle, *Politics and Development*, New Delhi: Sage Publications, 1998, pp.24-25.
9. Atul Kohli, *The State and Poverty in India: The Politics of Reform*, Cambridge: Cambridge University Press, 1987, p.3.
10. Keya Sengupta, *Genesis of Human Development in North-East India*, New Delhi: Concept Publishing Company, 2009, p.57.

11. United Nations, Report of the World Summit for Social Development 2005, United Nation,2 005.
12. This approach has been pioneered by Rowntree, 1901, and Booth, 1902, in Great Britain, see C., Seidl, Poverty Measurement: ASurvey, in D.Bos, M.Rose, C.Seidl (eds.), *Welfare and Efficiency in Public Economics*, New York: Springer, 1988, pp.71-147.
13. Debesh Bhowmik, *Economics of Poverty*, New Delhi: Deep & Deep Publications, 2007, p. 5.
14. J. Drewnowski, and W. Scott, *The Level of Living Index,* Geneva: United Nations Research Institute for Social Development (UNRISD), Report No. 4, 1966.
15. Seldon H. Danziger and Robert H. Haveman, *Understanding Poverty*, London: Harvard University Press, 1992, pp. 30-31; Ruth Lister, *Poverty*, UK: Polity Press, 2004, pp. 28-35.
16. This concept has been developed by Fieghen et al., Who Argued that With a Relative Definition of Poverty, see G.C. Fieghen, P. S. Lansley, A. D. Smith, *Poverty and Progress in Britain 1953-1973*, Cambridge: Cambridge University Press, 1977.
17. A segment of the population whose income falls within a certainrange, http://www.businessdictionary.com/definition/income-group.htmlixzz3pvblJLVC, accessed on October 9, 2015.
18. Diana Pearce, "The Feminization on of Poverty: Women, Work and Welfare", *Urban and Social Change Review*, 1978, pp. 28-38.
19. Fukuda Parr, "What does Feminization on of Poverty Mean? It isn't Just Lack of Income", *Feminist Economics*, 1999, p. 102.
20. V. M. Moghadam, "The Feminization of Poverty and Women's Human Rights", *Social and Human Sciences*, 2005, p. 4; www.unesco.org/shs/gender.
21. Poona Wignaraja, *Women Poverty and Resources*, New Delhi: Sage Publication, 1990.
22. Naila Kabeer, "Women's Economic Empowerment and Inclusive Growth: Labour Market and Enterprise

Development", Department for International Development and International Development Research Center, UK, Research Working Paper, 2003.

23. Govind Kelkar, "At the Threshold of Economic Empowerment: Women, Work and Gender Regimes in Asia", ILO Asia-Pacific Working Paper Series, 2013.
24. Note: Mass poverty is the poverty that affects the masses of a population who have extreme want of necessities. In general, mass poverty is an expression with broad implications that goes beyond the limitations of the amount of money or material possessions that the people have.
25. S. R., Hasim, "Dimensions of Poverty and Approach to Poverty Alleviation", *IASSI Quarterly*, Vol. 13, No.1, 1996, p. 20.
26. The Chronic Poverty Research Center, *The Chronic Poverty Report 2004-05*, Published by Manchester: UK, 2005.
27. Shenggen Fan, Peter Hazell, and Sukhadeo Thorat, "Government Spending, Growth and Poverty: An Analysis of Interlinkages in Rural India", EPTD Discussion Paper 33, Environment and Production Technology Division: International Food Policy Research Institute, 1998. pp.1-5.
28. http://planningcommission.nic.in, accessed on January 12, 2014.
29. Government of India, *Annual Report of 2010-11*, Planning Commission of India, 2011.
30. http://povertydata.worldbank.org/poverty/country/IND, accessed on February 12, 2014.
31. Government of India, *Economic Survey of India, 2011-2012*, Director of Economics and Statistics, 2011.
32. Yan Zhang, "Poverty Alleviation in China: Progress Policies and Implications for developing countries, in J. Hebel, Samadi, D. Nurrochmat (eds.), *Poverty Alleviation: Concepts and Experiences, focused on Indonesian Case*, Gottingen: Cuvillier Verlag, 2004, p. 60.
33. K. R. Bandyopadhyay, *Poverty Alleviation and Pro-Poor Growth in India*, New Delhi: Asian Institute of Transport Development, 2007.

34. Government of India, Economic Survey, Ministry of Finance, Government of India, Annual Report 2004-2005.
35. S. R., Hasim, "Dimensions of Poverty and Approach to Poverty Alleviation", *IASSI Quarterly*, Vol. 13, No.1, 1996, pp. 55-67; Naveen, Mishra, *Poverty in South Asia*, New Delhi: Authors Press, 2001; J. K. Galbraith, *The Nature of Mass Poverty*, New Delhi: Penguin books, 1984.
36. M. Adil Khan, *Economic Development, Poverty Alleviation and Governance: The Asian Experience,* New Delhi: Ashgate Publishing Limited, 1996.

3 Plans and Programme for Poverty Alleviation: A Critique

This overwhelming persistence of poverty in India has become a central question for planners and civil society. The Government of India had undertaken various significant steps for poverty alleviation in the beginning of the 50s through various Five Year Plans with a growth-oriented strategy for faster economic growth. Attempts at creating employment opportunities, development in the field of agriculture, health, education and other social services in order to alleviate poverty have since then occupied a prominent place in the public policy agenda of the Government of India.[1] In this direction, it is well known that massive efforts were made to bring about rapid and sustainable development and socio-economic transformation particularly in rural India with an integrated approach towards improving the quality of life of rural poor to ensure equity and effective peoples' participation.[2] There was also a move for de-bureaucratisation of poverty related programmes through peoples' participation at the grass-root level via Panchayati Raj Institutions. Currently, the poverty alleviation programmes predominantly focussed on people's participation and rural organisations as the key attributes for their success accompanied by equally important aspects, inter alia, concept of integrated development, planning process, growth center approach, management inputs, communication system and supporting management information system to improve the effectiveness of programmes and achieve the desired objectives of the programme. A number of schemes like Community Development Programme (CDP), National Extension Service (NES), Integrated Agricultural Development Programme (IADP), High Yielding Varieties Programme (HYVP) were adopted by the Government of India to address the poverty related problems and rural development.

The objectives of these programmes were to assist poor families in developing skills and generating employment to overcome poverty. Although, this strategy led to the increase in agricultural production, yet it was evident from various research works that these measures were not adequate to alleviate rural poverty and unemployment.

In addition to this, Planning Commission after the first decade of planning stated that 50 to 60 per cent of the rural population (aprox 211 million) could not afford minimum level of consumption, calculated primarily in terms of calories intake necessary to avoid the onset of malnutrition.[3] The development experiences of about 15 years (1951-1967) attributed to serious doubt about the assumption of the planners that strategies of growth and productivity will suffice in resolving the problems of rural poverty[4] as the problem of unemployment and underdevelopment still continues to be serious.

In the early 70s, there had been greater state intervention in the poverty alleviation through target-group oriented and area development programmes such as Small Farmers Development Agency (SFDA), Marginal Farmers and Agricultural Labour Scheme (MFALDA), Drought Prone Areas Programme (DPAP), Hill Areas Development Programme (HADP), Command Area Development Programme (CADP), etc. It was initiated on the recommendation of All India Rural Credit Review Committee (1969) that orderly and peaceful change in the rural economy would be troubled and effort to step up agricultural production would also be frustrated if the fruit of development continues to be denied to large section of the rural community.[5] In addition to this, various leading international organisations such as the World Bank (WB), International Labour Organisation (ILO), International Bank of Reconstruction and Development (IBRD), Food and Agricultural Organisation (FAO), World Health Organisation (WHO), International Fund for Agricultural Development (IFAD) as well as academician also come to question the approach to rural poverty. They also advocate the need of redirecting development policy through creation of employment opportunities, increasing investment and capital formation among poorer sections.[6] Therefore, poverty alleviation became a major objective in India during the 70s. It was a period marked by a more or less global stagnation on agricultural front. However, it was realised that the benefits of these programmes did not percolate down to the rural poor.[7]

In this connection, McNamara opined that the development effort of the past had not trickled down to the rural poor and there was need to formulate a new approach for rural development through growth and distributive justice. Further, he stated that one of the principle tasks for donor agencies was to fight against poverty. The poverty eradication slogan "Garibi Hatao" was also popularised during 70s by the then Prime Minister of India.[8] The attempt to address the issue of poverty even became a political manifesto of most of the political parties with slogans such as the "Roti, Kapda aur Makan" (food, clothes and shelter). It may be noted here that poverty alleviation schemes were used to gain political dividends by political leaders whose constituencies fall under the area of rural poor, Schedule Castes, Schedule Tribes (SCs&STs).[9] In the late 70s, a plea was made for improving productive assets by providing employment opportunities to the rural poor during the lean agricultural seasons of the year. Therefore, the seriousness on the part of the government with regard to removal of poverty became more visible during the 70s and 80s. This can be seen from the various programmes that were launched by the Government of India. These programmes have been broadly classified into four categories:

1. Self-employment programmes.
2. Wage employment programmes.
3. Public Distribution System (PDS) and nutrition programme, and
4. Social security programmes.[10]

Self-employment Programmes

The self-employment programmes were designed to provide skills subsidised credit and infrastructure support to small farmers and agricultural labourers. It started from late 70s in rural areas of the country with the name of Integrated Rural Development Programme (IRDP) to alleviate poverty as well as generate income especially for the poorer through generating substantial employment opportunities. Under this Act, 30 per cent priority was to be given to women. The major objective of this programme was to bring rural families in the identified target groups above the poverty line. The IRDP aimed at integration of five major sectors viz. (i) Agriculture including animal husbandry, fishery, forestry and horticulture; (ii) Cottage and small scale industries in villages; (iii) Tertiary sector which would cover artisans and the requirements of skilled workers in several rural activities; (iv) Employment in various services that was necessary for the achievement of production and distribution in the fields of comprehensive agriculture and rural industries; and (v) Labour mobilisation, training in skills and organised mobility to tie up labour with opportunity.

In addition, Training of Rural Youth for Self-Employment (TRYSEM), Development of Women and Children in Rural Areas (DWCRA), Supply of Improved Tool Kits to Rural Artisans (SITRA) and Ganga Kalyan Yojana (GKY) were also introduced as sub-programmes of IRDP to take care of the specific needs of the rural population. These schemes were implemented as 'stand-alone programmes', an approach which substantially detracted from their effectiveness.[11] Further, these programmes have been financed by government subsidies and bank credit, resulting in some changes in the lives of rural poor in terms of marginal improvement of their economic conditions as well as generation of additional income provided through employment opportunities. According to NABARD, about 47 per cent of respondents had been able to generate their family income through the scheme. However, according to the programme evaluation organisation reports, research studies conducted in various parts of the country and reports of central government show that IRDP could not fully succeed in satisfying the aspirations of the rural poor[12] due to over-crowding of projects, lack of bank credit, lack of market linkages, etc.

Further, the marginal impact of self-employment programmes led to the constitution of S.R. Hassam Committee by the Planning Commission in 1977 to review self-employment programmes. The committee recommended the merger of all self-employment programmes for the rural poor and a shift from the individual beneficiary approach to a group-based approach. In 1999, therefore, IRDP was merged with DWCRA, TRYSEM and other allied programmes including the Million Wells Scheme (MWS), namely

Swarnajayanti Gram Swarojgar Yojana (SGSY). The SGSY is the major on-going programme for the self-employment of rural poor.

SGSY programme is rooted in the belief that rural poor in India have potentialities to produce valuable goods and services if right support is given in this direction. The major objective of the SGSY was to bring the assisted poor families above the poverty line by providing them income-generating assets through bank credit and governmental subsidy. Families from the Below Poverty Line (BPL) in rural areas constitute the target group of the SGSY. Within the target group, special safeguards have been provided to vulnerable sections, by way of reserving 50 per cent benefits for SCs / STs, 40 per cent for women and 3 per cent for disabled persons. It was expected to directly help SHGs to establish sustainable micro-enterprises for self-employment at the grass-root level by providing sustainable income as the SHGs are seen as a viable alternative for achieving the targets for rural development and getting community participation in poverty alleviation programmes. Further, social mobilisation enables the poor to build their own organisations to participate directly in decisions that would enable them to overcome poverty. The SGSY is being implemented by the District Rural Development Agency (DRDA) with the active involvement of Panchayati Raj Institutions (PRIs), the Banks, the Line Departments and the Non-Government Organisations (NGOs). Therefore, the SGSY programme is perceived as a scheme for greater equality and justice and a more realistic measure for the upliftment of the rural poor.

Critique of the above mentioned self-employment programmes, however, proved to be inadequate in substantially alleviating poverty. The concept of self-employment is mostly concentrated on grants and subsidies. This concept fails to stimulate self-reliance and leads to habit of dependence. It was said that the self-employment programmes have failed to achieve the desired objectives due to the absence of planning of suitable projects, lack of skilled beneficiaries with experience in managing an enterprise, defective delivery of credit by banks and wrong selection of beneficiaries. According to Rath, self-employment programmes are not realistic, as the households are least capable of self-employment and also, because the economy too does not have adequate productive assets for distribution among the poor. It is necessary to understand the specific characteristics of rural society which give rise to the problems of poverty in rural areas.

Wage Employment Programmes

Wage employment programmes, an important component of the anti-poverty strategy, provide livelihood during the lean agricultural season as well as during droughts, floods and other natural calamities. These programmes put an upward pressure on market wage rates by attracting people to public works' programmes. Wage employment programmes not only provide employment to the villagers but also create a village infrastructure, such as deepening village ponds, constructing village schools and rural roads. These programmes were first started during the 6th and 7th Five Year Plan in the form of National Rural Employment Programme (NREP) and Rural Landless Employment Guarantee Programmes (RLEGP). Several wage employment programmes are Jawahar Rozgar Yojana (JRY), Employment Assurance Scheme (EAS), Sampoorna Grameen Rojgar Yojana (SGRY), Pradhan Mantri Gramodaya Yojana (PMGY), Assam Bikash Yojana (ABY), etc.

JRY was started in 1989 by merging NREP and RLEGP; it was designed to generate gainful employment for the unemployed and under-employed persons in rural areas through the creation of economic infrastructure and social assets. Besides these objectives, it also aimed to improve the standard of living and the level of wages for which priority should be given to the SCs / STs and women. The programme was introduced in 120 identified backward districts in 12 states of the country with a target of providing 90-100 days of employment per person in areas where there was a concentration of unemployed and under-employed persons. In addition, JRY was introduced for taking up special and innovative projects aimed at preventing migration of labourers, enhancing women's employment and undertaking special programmes through voluntary organisations for drought proofing areas. According to the government reports, 73,764,83 lakh man-days of employment were generated and about 47 per cent of STs / SCs, 36 per cent landless labourers were benefitted through this programme till 1989-1999.[13] However, several studies account that the implementation of JRY was slow due to lack of co-ordination at the different levels and line departments. Further, EAS was introduced in 1993 covering 1,778 drought-prone, desert, tribal and hill areas blocks of the country to provide gainful employment during lean agricultural seasons to adults and creation of economic infrastructure, community assets for sustained employment and development in rural areas. Although, the scheme was demand-driven, self-targeting in nature and open to rural poor who are in need of employment at minimum wage rates, however, resources were allocated to states based on the incidence of poverty. A maximum of two adult per family would be provided wage employment, when there is demand during lean agricultural season. Although EAS has played a major role in protecting consumption patterns of the rural poor during natural calamities, scholars have revealed that this programme has failed to generate employment to the beneficiaries due to political interference and lack of will. Therefore, all the wage employment programmes i.e. NREP, RLEGP and JRY were merged into one programme in 2001 called SGSY to break the cycle of unemployment and food insecurity by providing employment during the lean agricultural season through creating rural infrastructure with a desire to supplement their primary income by providing unskilled manual work and also laid special emphasis on women, Scheduled Castes (SCs), Scheduled Tribes (STs) and parents of children withdrawn from hazardous occupations. SGSY was implemented through the Panchayati Raj Institutions, line departments' and NGOs.

Further, Pradhan Mantri Gramodaya Yojana was introduced in 2000-2001 with the aim of sustainable development and poverty alleviation in the rural areas by creating social and economic infrastructure with the objectives of improving the quality of rural life to provide better health care, drinking water, nutrition, education, shelter, etc. Apart from these national schemes, the Assam government too initiated certain poverty alleviation programmes i.e. Assam Bikash Yojana, to create employment opportunities through distribution of employment generating assets with subsidy to unemployed youth of both rural and urban areas of the state.

A review of various wage employment programmes during the 9th Five Year Plan shows that there has been a considerable reduction in terms of allocation of resources for employment generation largely due to changes in allocation for poverty alleviation programmes. Moreover, the wage employment programmes provide only short-term relief to the poor.[14] Long-term sustainable poverty reduction in the underdeveloped region can come about only if other sectors of economy grow rapidly. However, in Indian context, agricultural growth still holds the key to poverty alleviation and there is considerable scope for increasing agricultural productivity through expansion of irrigation, better land and water management practices and infrastructure support.

Public Distribution System (PDS) and Nutrition Programmes

Food security is largely addressed by the Public Distribution System (PDS). The main objective of the programme is to meet the basic needs of the access to food by rural poor. The PDS is a safety net programme open to all citizens and an instrument for improving food security at the household level in India where millions of poor are crippled by chronic poverty and malnutrition. Earlier, PDS was mainly meant for urban population but in recent years it also covered rural population.[15] The PDS was introduced in 1997 under which special cards were issued to families Below Poverty Line (BPL) and food grains were distributed at a lower price to these families compared to those Above the Poverty Line (APL). The entire population was divided into three categories viz. BPL (Below Poverty Line), APL (Above Poverty Line) and AAY (Antyodaya Anna Yojana). The BPL and AAY population were provided food grains per month at subsidised price (35 kg of food grains at Rs 2 per kg). Although, this programme had over the time been recognised as an important poverty alleviation programme because it has provided food grains at reasonably low costs to help them improve their nutrition standards and attain food security.

Social Security Programmes

Social security programme viz; National Social Assistance Programme (NSAP) is meant for those who are at the bottom of the BPL facing destitution and desertion. The NSAP launched in 1995 marks a significant step towards fulfilment of the Directive Principle of State Policy by ensuring a minimum national standard of social assistance for the poor. NSAP is comprised of schemes like Indira Gandhi National Old Age Pension Scheme (IGNOAPS), Indira Gandhi National Widow Pension Scheme (IGNWPS), Indira Gandhi National Disability Pension Scheme (IGNDPS), National Family

Benefit Scheme (NFBS) and Annapurna.[16] The IGNOAPS provides a monthly pension of Rs 75 to destitute BPL persons above the age of 65. The NFBS is a scheme for BPL families who are given Rs 10,000 in the case of the death of the bread-winner. The aim of NMBS is to provide Rs 500 to support nutritional intake for pregnant women. The National Old Age Pension Scheme (NOAPS) and the Annapurna were launched in 2002 to provide food security to senior citizens who, though eligible for old age pensions, remain uncovered under NOAPS. However, it was pointed out by scholars that the coverage of NSAP is very limited in the rural areas of the country due to limited resources and lack of supervision.

With regard to PDS and social security programmes, numbers of studies have been conducted. It was said that the PDS and social security programmes could not provide maximum benefits to the poor in order to alleviate poverty because of limited information, weakness in the delivery system, poor quality of food grains, creation of illegal ration cards and failure of credit to reach the poor.

Experience of various poverty alleviation programmes such as self-employment programmes, wage employment programmes, public distribution system and social security programmes have been criticised for failing to provide social security to the rural poor due to shortcomings in the programmes design and administrative weaknesses. It was observed that earlier poverty alleviation programmes were only focussed on the concept of underdeveloped / development, but ignored some of the important requirements of development like capability expansion of individuals and communities, participation of people, etc. Moreover, there were deficiencies in institutional capability in delivery and corruption in implementation of these schemes, thereby causing the failure of most of the above cited poverty alleviation programmes. Further, Bagchee while reviewing the poverty alleviation programmes found that the programmes did not achieve structured objectives due to the absence of conceptual clarity and an inadequate understanding of the complex nature of the environment because of which poverty in the rural areas still prevails in India.[17] It may be noted here that the poverty alleviation programmes failed due to lack of capability of the delivery system and utilisation of resources in an efficient manner.

The programmes are more or less focussed on project approach or a sectoral approach which is not adequate to alleviate poverty of the rural area and distribution of benefits to local population, mainly the weaker sections of the society. The magnitude of unemployment and poverty and the potential for development of farm and non-farm sector varies widely among regions and also within regions. The efforts have to be made to make the programmes area specific and utilise the local endowments for growth, social justice and full employment. Besides, effort has to be made to plan for integration of various programmes and establish appropriate linkages for optimal utilisation of local endowments consistent with the plan objectives, local needs/aspirations and environmental balance.

References

1. R. Radhakrishna and Shovan Ray, *Handbook of Poverty in India*: Perspectives, Policies, and Programmes, New Delhi: Oxford University Press, 2005, p.1.
2. K.R. Gupta, *Rural Development in India*, Vol. 2, New Delhi: Atlantic Publishers, 2003, p.384.
3. Perspective Planning Division, Prospective of Development: 1961-1976, *Implication of Planning for a Minimum Level of Living*, Planning Commission, Government of India, New Delhi, 1962, pp. 4-5.
4. Kuldeep Mathur, "Designing Poverty Alleviation Programmes: International Agencies and Indian Politics", (ed.), *Development Policy and Administration*, New Delhi: Sage Publications, 1996, pp.181-182.
5. Ibid., p.182.
6. A. Vaidyanathan, *India's Economic Reform and Development,* New Delhi: Academic Foundation, 2003, p. 215.
7. S.N. Misra, *Poverty Alleviation Programmes and Gram Panchayats*, New Delhi: Mittal Publications, 1997, *Food and Nutritional Security: Role of Food Assistance in India*, Compilation of Papers from WFP State Consultation, New Delhi: Lancer Publishers and Distributors, 2006.
8. D. N. Dwivedi, *Economic Concentration and Poverty in India,* New Delhi: Datta Book Centre, 1974, pp.67-69.

9. Atul Kohli, *The State and Poverty in India: The Politics of Reform*, Cambridge: Cambridge University Press, 1987, pp. 23-24.
10. C.A.K. Yesudian, Poverty Alleviation Programme in India: A Social Audit, Mumbai, *Indian Journal of Medical Research*, Vol. 126, 2007, pp.364-373.
11. Planning Commission, *Tenth Five Year Plan 2002-2007*, Sectoral Policies and Programmes, Government of India, Vol. II, 2009, pp. 294-295.
12. http://planningcommission.nic.in/plans/mta/mta-9702/mta-ch6.pdf, accessed on December 13, 2012.
13. K. R. Gupta, Poverty Alleviation in Rural India: Strategy and Programmes (ed.), *Poverty in India*, NewDelhi: Atlantic Publishers and Distributors, 2008, pp.170-172.
14. K. Seeta Prabhu and R. Sudarshan, *Reforming India's Social Sector: Poverty Nutrition, Health and Education,* New Delhi: Social Science Press, 2002, pp.53-54.
15. Ananth S. Panth, Social Network and Food Security in Rural Karnataka, *Economic Political Weekly*, Vol.32, No, 12 April, 1997, pp. 756-758.
16. http://nsap.nic.in/, accessed on February 20, 2012.
17. Sandeep Bagchee, "Poverty Alleviation Programmes in Seventh Plan-An Appraisal", *Economic and Political Weekly*, Vol. 22, No. 4, January 24, 1987, pp.139-148.

4 MGNREGA: A Rights-Based Policy

Introduction

Mahatma Gandhi National Rural Employment Guarantee Act offered a paradigm shift in the strategy of wage employment programmes to address the shortcomings of earlier poverty alleviation programmes. This programme attempts to address the key concerns related to poverty in India i.e. unemployment and a flagging agriculture sector.[1] In order to address these problems, the present policy-frame is based on three-pronged accomplishment to alleviate and reduce poverty in the country which constitutes:

a) Stepping up of economic growth;

b) Direct strike on poverty through employment, income-generating programmes and assets creation for the poor; and,

c) Human and social development policies for the poor.[2]

National Rural Employment Guarantee Act (NREGA) which is subsequently renamed as Mahatma Gandhi National Rural Employment Guarantee Act in the year 2009-10, is a wage employment programme and the ongoing programmes of Sampurna Gramin Rojgar Yojana (SGRY) and National Food for Work (NFFW) are subsumed in MGNREGA. The scheme is funded by the Central Government of India, which creates a 'right to work' for all households in the rural India. MGNREGA has been introduced to transform rural India into a more productive, equitable and connected society by providing employment opportunities to the rural poor. This programme gives great hope to alleviate poverty in rural areas. It was enacted on September 7, 2005, with the objectives of "enhancement of livelihood security of the rural household by providing at least

100 days of guaranteed wage employment in every financial year to an adult member of any rural household willing to do unskilled manual work at the statutory minimum wage". It is a demand-based programme through the Gram Sabha. The Act came into effect from February 2, 2006. MGNREGA was implemented in a phased manner with 200 districts in the first phase, followed by another 130 districts from April 2007 and in the remaining districts, with effect from April 2008. The Act is now effective in the rural areas of the entire country covering 619 districts. During the first year of implementation (Financial Year 2006-07) in 200 districts, 2.10 crore households were employed and 90.5 crore person-days were generated. In 2007-08, 3.39 crore households were provided employment and 143.59 crore person-days were generated in 330 districts. In 2008-09, 4.51 crore households were provided employment and 216.32 crore person-days had been generated across the country.[3] Further, almost 50 per cent of the Drought Prone Areas Programme (DPAP)[4] districts were included under MGNREGA indicating that the scheme can have some contribution towards rain-fed areas.[5]

The most significant features of the Act are that it is seen to be designed to allow women equity in both access to work and in the payment of wages. The Act mandates that at least one-third of the workers should be women. Independent studies like the one conducted by Indian Institute of Management, Bangalore, have indicated that with the implementation of MGNREGA, out-migration from villages has decreased. Migration from tribal areas has also substantially declined due to MGNREGA in several districts like Dungarpur, Udaipur, Jhabua, Dhar, etc.[6] Various field studies done by the researchers[7] shows that states like Orissa, Sikkim, Tripura and Goa have been able to reduce poverty over the past five years. Further, it is said that MGNREGA has helped rural households in a sustained manner to balance consumption between the agricultural peak season and lean season.

Objectives of MGNREGA

a) Ensuring social protection for the most vulnerable people living in rural India through providing employment opportunities.

b) Ensuring livelihood security for the poor through creation of durable assets, improved water security, soil conservation and higher land productivity.

c) Strengthening drought-proofing and flood management in rural India.

d) Empowerment of the marginalised communities, especially women, Scheduled Castes (SCs) and Scheduled Tribes (STs), through the processes of a rights-based legislation.

e) Strengthening decentralised, participatory planning through convergence of various anti-poverty and livelihoods' initiatives.

f) Deepening democracy at the grass-roots by strengthening the Panchayati Raj Institutions (PRIs)

g) Effecting greater transparency and accountability in governance.

Salient Features of MGNREGA

MGNREGA is a powerful instrument for inclusive growth in rural India through social protection, livelihood security and democratic empowerment. It goes beyond poverty alleviation and recognises employment as a legal right. Several studies show that due to its self-selecting demand driven design, MGNREGA is able to engage with the most vulnerable and marginalised section of the society. Further, it has opened up opportunities for large-scale employment of skilled manpower at the block/village levels in rural areas through large-scale deployment of mates, engineers, village assistants, accountants, IT personnel, etc. This scheme provides an additional incentive for states to leverage the Act to meet the employment needs of the poor. MGNREGA also marks a break from the relief programmes of the past towards an integrated natural resource management and livelihood generation perspective.

Further, to effectively address the issue of poverty alleviation, the Ministry of Rural Development emphasise on 'convergence of MGNREGA with other schemes. The major focus of the convergence is better achievement of the scheme's aims and objectives in creation of durable assets, securing livelihood of rural households and encouraging the states. The convergence has enhanced efforts through inter-sectoral approaches and different programmes such as Watershed Programmes, National Agriculture Development Programme (Rashtriya Krishi Vikas Yojana), National Horticulture Mission, Scheme of Artificial Recharge of Ground Water through dug well, BRGF, with MGNREGA that enable better planning and effective investments in rural areas. This convergence has brought in synergies between different government programmes / schemes in terms of planning, process and implementation. The salient features of the Act are as follows:

Registration: To join under MGNREGA, every household has to submit their application with their names, age and address to the Gram Panchayat at the village level for registration. All adult members of the household who attain the age of 18 years can register and apply for work and the applications for registration are given in plain paper to the Gram Panchayat (GP).

Issuing of Job Card: The job card is a basic physical instrument that enables an applicant to demand for work. Job cards are issued within 15 days of registration or submission of application after the verification of the place of residence and age of the applicants. The job card contains the details of an adult member along with enrolment number and his / her photo.

Application for Work: After the issuing of job card, the job card holder has to submit a written application for employment to the GP or to the Programme Officer (PO) at the block level. The Gram Panchayat or Programme Officer is to be issued a dated receipt of the written application for employment, against the guarantee of providing employment within 15 days of demand.

Unemployment Allowances: As per the Act, if employment is not provided within 15 days from the date of application of demand for work, the state has to pay an unemployment allowance to the job card holders.

Provision and Execution of Work: While allocating work, there are some provisions of work under MGNREGA where work is provided within 5 km radius of the village. In case, work is provided beyond 5 km, extra wages of 10 per cent are payable to meet additional transportation and living expenses.

Further, all work taken up by the Gram Panchayats, the cost of the material component including the wages of the skilled and semi-skilled workers shall not exceed 40 per cent at the Gram Panchayat level. Allocation of funds in the ratio of 60:40 for unskilled and semi-skilled / material components of the work ensures the primacy of labour intensive nature of work. Worksite facilities such as crèche, drinking water and shade have to be provided at all work sites. Further, to ensure that the workers are directly benefited under the scheme, the Act prohibits the use of contractors or machinery in execution of the work.

Payment of Wages: Payment of wages is paid to the beneficiaries as per State-wise Government of India (GOI) under the Minimum Wage Act, 1948, unless the wages have been notified by the central government under Section 6(1) of the Act. Again, it is recommended that equal wages to be paid to both male and female workers as per the provisions of the Equal Remuneration Act, 1976. Under MGNREGA, wages are to be paid to the beneficiaries within 15 days from the closure date of the muster roll. Further, payment of wages has to be mandatorily done through the beneficiaries' individual / joint bank / post-office account. As per the Act, third party is not allowed to withdraw money from the bank without the due authorisation of the workers in writing. All data regarding the payment of wages are recorded in the job card. The types of bank allowed are rural bank, cooperative bank, nationalised bank and mobile banks for inaccessible areas.

Social Audit: An innovative feature of MGNREGA is that it gives a central role to 'Social Audit' that is being introduced for the first time in any public expenditure programmes as a means of continuous public vigilance. It is meant to be an effective means for ensuring transparency and accountability under MGNREGA. Social audit is conducted by Gram Shaba once in six months of all the projects under the scheme taken up within the Gram Panchayat. It includes information regarding the registration of families, issue of job cards, receipts of work application, allotment of work, payment of wages, unemployment allowances and supervision of work.

Awareness Generation: With regard to awareness generation, the state government has undertaken initiatives like Information and Communication Technology (ICT) exercise to publicise the key provision of MGNREGA such as process of registration, demand for employment, unemployment allowances, grievance redressal and social audit. Under, ICT, the Act set up a toll free national helpline for the protection of workers' entitlements and rights. The state government draws up an ICT plan and developed communication material designed to help people articulate their demand and claim their entitlements. The information is widely disseminated, especially in remote areas through television, radio, films, print, and media including vernacular newspaper, pamphlets and brochures.

Grievance Redressal: The Ministry of Rural Development has accorded utmost importance to the organisation of ombudsmen in each district to consider complaints relating to the implementation of MGNREGA and take legal action. The state government is responsible for appointing ombudsman on the recommendation of selection committee.

Further, the transparency and accountability mechanisms under MGNREGA create a scope for unprecedented accountability of performance, especially towards immediate stakeholders. Some of its other unique features are:

1. Formulation and implementation of development plans follow a bottom-up approach at all three PRI tiers. This approach is supported by a strong technical system at all levels.
2. MGNREGA adopts an integrated national rural management approach towards focussing on sustainability. It focusses on rational utilisation of land, water and forest to achieve and sustain potential agricultural productivity.

In 2011, the Ministry of Rural Development released a discussion paper entitled *Reforms in MGNREGA Implementation* that identified the following challenges in the MGNREGA implementation:

1. Ensure demand-driven legal entitlements.
2. Reduce distress migration from rural areas.
3. Reduce delays in wage payments to workers.
4. Provide the requisite number of days of work as per demand.
5. Improve quality of assets created under MGNREGA.
6. Ensure full payment of wages stipulated under MGNREGA.

7. Anchor participatory grass-root planning.
8. Sustain regular flow of funds.
9. Strengthen grievance redressal mechanisms.

To deal with the above-stated challenges, the central government set up an expert committee under the chairmanship of Dr Mihir Shah, Member, Planning Commission. The committee recommended to strengthen the synergy between MGNREGA and agriculture and allied rural livelihoods, to respond to the demands of the states for greater location specific flexibility in permissible works and to improve the ecological balance in rural India and to provide a cleaner, healthier environment for the rural population. Further, it includes strengthening the demand-driven character of the programme, preparation of labour budget, strict time-schedules, adequate human resources, expanded list of permissible works, reducing delays in payments, greater role for civil society and strengthening social audits, vigilance and grievance redressal.

The committee has also suggested that all payments under MGNREGA be made within 15 days and interim payments be allowed in cases where measurement of work has not been finished. Delay in payment should be considered a punishable offence under section 25 of the Act. It has listed some new activities which include rice cultivation using the System of Rice Intensification (SRI), soil conservation activities, production of manure and bio-pesticides, construction of seed-storage bins and shelters for cattle and poultry. The additional list of permissible works under MGNREGA have been grouped as those related to watershed in mountainous / plain area, agriculture, livestock, fishery, rural drinking water, rural sanitation and works in coastal areas.

MGNREGA, thus, can be considered as a People's Act and an important step towards the realisation of right to work. The Act ensures gender equality and working people's fundamental right to life with dignity. Further, it addresses the causes of chronic poverty such as drought, deforestation and soil erosion. The Act also empowers the ordinary people by providing employment opportunities as well as financial support to the needy and encourages people's participation in the planning and implementation of the scheme through Gram Panchayat, social audit, etc.

Table 4.1: Overall Performance of MGNREGA in Assam.

Sl. No.	Particular	FY 2015-16	FY 2016-17	FY 2017- 18 (up to January)
1.	Labour budget (in Lakh)	432.74	408	500
2.	Estimated labour budget (in Lakh)	326.64	317.67	450
3.	Person days generated (in Lakh)	372.71	376.84	411.73
4.	Percentage against proportionate labour budget	114.11	118.63	91.49
5.	Person days generated (in Lakh)	486.33	467.01	431.49
6.	Percentage against total labour budget (in Lakh)	112.38	114.46	86.30
7.	HHs provided employment (in Lakhs)	15.02	15.72	15.73
8.	Individuals worked (in Lakhs)	21.73	23.34	24.42
9.	Average days of employment per HH	--	32.37	29.72
10.	Percentage of women person days	--	33.59	36.45
11.	HHs completed 100 days of employment (in Nos.)	--	42,233	11,429
12.	HHs completed more than 100 days of employment	--	Nil	Nil

Source: nrega.nic.in

MGNREGA in Assam

MGNREGA was introduced in the State of Assam in seven districts on February 2, 2006, in the first phase. The second phase of MGNREGA covering six districts started in the year 2007 and the third phase started in April 2008 encompassing the remaining 14 districts of Assam. In the first phase covering 7 District of Assam, 323.70 lakh person-days were generated under MGNREGA. Further, in the second phase, it generated 133.25 lakh person-days covering 4 districts and in the third phase, 276.00 lakh person-days generated covering 14 districts. Moreover, during the FY 2010-11, across Assam, 37 lakh households had got job cards under MGNREGA and 16,473 households got jobs for 100 days. Independent studies conducted by the Northeast Social Trust indicated that 43,69,372 households in the state were provided job cards, whereas only 17,98,372 households got jobs in the year 2011-12. That means 58.84 per cent job card holders did not get any opportunity of working under MGNREGA. Through this scheme as many as 12.60988 million households were provided employment in Assam, out of which 298.53 million person-days were generated during the FY 2013-14. However, the corresponding percentage of women participation was only 24.75 under this scheme, which was very low.

According to the CAG report, only 9.03 per cent of the registered household in Assam got employment for 100 days from 2007 to 2012. Table 4.1 reflects the overall performance of MGNREGA during the year from 2015-16 to 2017-18. The table shows that the performance of MGNREGA has been significant in quantitative terms during that period. In Assam, around 15.2 lakh households were provided employment during the FY 2016-17. Table 4.2 shows the financial progress under MGNREGA in Assam.

Table 4.2: Financial Progress under MGNREGA in Assam.

Sl. No.	Particular	FY 2016-2017	FY 2017- 2018
1.	Release funds from Central Govt. (Rs. in Cr)	115659.79	111388.14
2.	Matching State share	11727.22	13269.56
3.	Total availability (Rs. in Cr)	168931.41	143940.88
4.	Total expenditure [Rs. in Cr]	1501.14	1277.83
5.	Wages expenditure [Rs. in Cr]	1255.51	813.09
6.	Material (%)	11.45	35.78
7.	Admin expenditure (%)	5.5	100
8.	Notified MGNREG wage rate (Rs.)	182	183
9.	Average wage rate per day per person (Rs.)	181.96	182.96
10.	Average cost per day per person (Rs.)	258.13	184.7
11.	Total Expenditure through e-payment (%)	100	100
12.	Payments generated within 15 days (%)	62.27	81

Source: nrega.nic.in

Women Participation under MGNREGA

With regard to women participation, studies have shown that all India participation of women under MGNREGA has increased marginally from 40 per cent of the total workforce in 2006-07 to 53 per cent in 2012-13. Various field studies done by the researchers shows that States like Kerela (93 per cent), Pondicherry (84 per cent), Goa (81 per cent) and Tamil Nadu (75 per cent) have highest percentage of participation under MGNREGA.

At the national level, participation of women has increased significantly from 46.41 per cent in 2010-11 to 48.81 per cent in 2011-12 and further to 53.01 per cent in 2012-13 which are exceeding expectations and the stipulated 33 per cent share. The share of women was less in States like Bihar, Punjab, West Bengal and most of northeastern states of India. However, in Assam, the participation of women beneficiaries is less than the stipulated percentage of one-third of the total MGNREGA workers. The participation rate of women in northeastern states of India is mentioned in the Table 4.3 below.

Table 4.3: Participation of Women under MGNREGA in Northeast India.

		Women Participation Rate (%)				
Sl.No.	**States**	**2013-14**	**2014-15**	**2015-16**	**2016-17**	**2017-18**
1.	Assam	24.75	28.13	33.59	36.45	38.72
2.	Meghalaya	41.62	42.53	44.93	44.28	46.39
3.	Mizoram	30.16	40.37	37.61	35.26	33.7
4.	Manipur	35.25	38.27	37.26	41.74	43.11
5.	Nagaland	28.93	31.21	31.28	29.68	28.61
6.	Arunachal Pradesh	30.35	30.17	31.64	34.1	35.41
7.	Sikkim	44.76	48.12	47.57	47.88	47.86
8.	Tripura	47.11	49.36	50.11	49.05	47.13

Source: nrega.nic.in

MGNREGA has been implemented with a lot of enthusiasm and initiatives. In Assam, rural connectivity, land development and flood control have been given more importance to maintain and develop rural connectivity by enhancing land productivity and connecting remote villages as well as by improving rural infrastructure. It is observed that since its inception, the state received overwhelming response from the rural poor regarding MGNREGA as it assists to eradicate rural unemployment and improving the living conditions of the poor and other vulnerable sections of society.

MGNREGA in Nalbari District

MGNREGA was implemented in Nalbari district in the FY 2007-08. According to information obtained from DRDA, in Nalbari, about 61,224 households demanded employment, out of them 51,105 households got employment during the first year of implementation. Further, only 270 households got job for 100 days. Official records relating to household participation under MGNREGA show that very few households got jobs for 100 days in a year. Although during the FY 2011-12, 10,3,912 job cards were issued, only 26,482 households had actually demanded employment and out of them only 4,861 households across Nalbari district got employment, out of which only 39 households got job for 100 days (reasons discussed in subsequent chapters). It is also to be noted that the participation of women under MGNREGA has declined over the years.

Data relating to employment provided to women under MGNREGA shows that very few women beneficiaries had got employment during the financial year 2013-14.Further, a total number of 23,245 households were provided employment under MGNREGA out of which only 3,198 women got employment during the same period. That means only 13.7 per cent of total women beneficiaries got employment in Nalbari district. Thus, to meet the objectives of the scheme given in the guidelines i.e. to bring gender equity by providing 33 per cent beneficiaries should be women, did not take place in Nalbari district. Further, the coverage of marginalised sections like STs/SCs and disabled was found to be very limited (Table 4.4.).

Table 4.4 :Participation under MGNREGA in Nalbari District.

Year	HH issued job cards	HH demanded employment	HH participation	HH completed 100 days	Person days in lakhs				
					SCs	STs	Other	Women	Total
2009-10	96766	69073	14683	509	89.3	227.37	416.57	203.5	19.64
2010-11	99101	50379	14413	303	1.68	1.09	10.04	0.81	12.81
2011-12	103912	26482	4861	39	31106	22973	634497	83348	688576
2012-13	103997	17152	2382	50	25326	12029	430787	53881	468142
2013-14	105225	24352	5655	82	20158	17255	495658	71253	533071

Table 4.5: Block-wise Employment provided to Women under MGNREGA in Nalbari District in 2013-14.

Sl. No	Block	Employment provided to women	Total
1	Borigog Banbhag	373	3550
2	Barkhetri	737	3602
3	Borbhag	175	3155
4	Madhupur	209	2108
5	Paschim Nalbari	637	4075
6	Pub-Nalbari	719	4442
7	Tihu	348	2313
	Total	**3,198**	**23,245**

Source: nrega.nic.in

As per MGNREGA guidelines, there were various works taken up such as water conservation, drought proofing (including afforestation and tree plantation), irrigation, renovation of traditional water bodies, land development, flood control, rural connectivity in terms of all-weather roads etc. Official records show that work related to rural connectivity and land development had got priority under the scheme in Nalbari district.

Table 4.6: Year-wise completed work under MGNREGA in Nalbari District of Assam from 2012-13 to 2013-14.

Sl. No.	Types of work	Financial Year	
		2012-13	**2013-14**
1.	Rural Connectivity	637	748
2.	Land Development	369	458
3.	Micro- Irrigation	42	77
4.	Water Conservation	110	46
5	Drought Proofing	407	83
6.	Traditional Water Bodies	56	57
7.	Flood Control	44	53

Source: nrega.nic.in

During the FY 2013-14, statistics of completed work under MGNREGA was 748 under rural connectivity, 458 under land development, 77 under micro-irrigation, 46 under water harvesting, 83 under drought proofing and 57 number of works were completed under renovation of traditional water bodies. Further, official record shows that highest number of MGNREGA works i.e. 1,024 works have been completed during the FY 2011-12 in Nalbari district (Table 4.7).

Table 4.7: Block-wise completed work under MGNREGA in Nalbari District from 2009-10 to 2013-14.

Sl. No	Block	2009-10	2010-11	2011-12	2012-13	2013-14
1.	Borigog Banbhag	140	97	313	61	93
2.	Barkhetri	153	40	95	56	98
3.	Borbhag	103	58	108	42	69
4.	Madhupur	82	35	78	37	89
5.	Paschim Nalbari	143	68	117	59	119
6.	Pub-Nalbari	117	44	245	74	173
7.	Tihu	116	17	68	32	48
8.	Total	854	359	1,024	361	689

Source: nrega.nic.in

As per the Act, funds are released to the districts on the basis of labour budget to the MGNREGA account by the Ministry of Rural Development. It was released after examining previous year's utilisation of funds. The labour budget is based on realistic estimate for the number of works to be taken up, as derived from the annual Shelf of Projects (SoPs) in the development plan.

Table 4.8: Year-wise Total Fund disbursed (labour expenditure and material expenditure) under MGNREGA in Nalbari District from 2008-09 to 2015-16.

Sl. No.	Year	Labour expenditure (in lakhs)	Material expenditure (in lakhs)
1.	2008-09	2,303	1,011
2.	2009-10	1,825	883
3.	2010-11	1,332	819
4.	2011-12	NA	NA
5.	2012-13	658	216
6.	2013-14	814	358
7.	2014-15	368	140
8.	2015-16	223	109

Source: nrega.nic.in

From the above Table 4.8, it was observed that fund disbursed under MGNREGA varies from year to year. It is also observed that very less amount of fund is released in the district which may be due to delay in submission of utilisation of funds to the central government and lack of co-ordination among the implementing officials.

Various poverty alleviation programmes, however, proved to be inadequate in substantially alleviating poverty, therefore, MGNREGA is meant to be an example of demand-driven and gender-sensitive scheme with nationwide coverage and social protection measure which provides a minimum income alongside stimulating local development. MGNREGA was expected to generate income and enhance the capability vector of individuals and communities. Further, to ensure transparency and accountability, social audit and ombudsmen is enabled under MGNREGA for monitoring and analysing the quality of work as well as to mobilise awareness among the rural people.

References

1. Rebecca Holmes, Nidhi Sadana and Saswatee Rath, "An Opportunity for Change? Gender Analysis of the Mahatma Gandhi National Rural Employment Guarantee Act," Working Paper, No. 53, Overseas Development Institution, 2011, pp. 1-4.
2. Government of India, *The National Rural Employment Guarantee Act 2005, Operational Guidelines,* Ministry of Rural Development, New Delhi, 2005, pp.1-2.
3. http://nrega.nic.in, accessed on July 25, 2014.
4. Drought Prone Areas Programme (DPAP) is the earliest area development programme launched by the central government in 1973-74 to tackle the special problems faced by fragile areas that are constantly affected by severe drought conditions.
5. Amita Sharma, "Right Based Legal Guarantee as Development Policy: The Mahatma Gandhi National Rural Employment Guarantee Act", India: UNDP, 2010, p.9.
6. Ministry of Rural Development, Government of India, *Report of the Committee for Revision of MGNREGA*

Operational Guideline, edited by Mihir Shah, New Delhi: Ministry of Rural Development, 2009, p.2.

7. Birendra Suna, Sanjay Pratap and Anand Kumar, "Responding to People's Protests about Poverty: Making and Implementation of the National Rural Employment Guarantee Act in India," Paper Presented at the International Conference at Manchester University, 2010.

5 Implementation Mechanism and MGNREGA

The state agencies play a significant role in the implementation of various poverty alleviation programmes in the rural areas of India. These agencies are responsible for monitoring and evaluating the anti-poverty programmes. In states with better administrative mechanism as well as governance, they play an effective role for the implementation in the scheme. The guidelines of Mahatma Gandhi National Rural Employment Guarantee Act also sought to involve large number of stakeholders from the village level to central level such as Panchayati Raj Institutions especially Gram Panchayat (GP) and Gram Sabha (GS) at village level; Programme Officers (PO) and Anchalik Panchayat at block level; Zila Parishad (ZP) and District Programme Coordinator (DPC) at the district level; State Employment Guarantee Council (SEGC) and State Government at the State level; Central Employment Guarantee Council (CEGC) and Ministry of Rural Development (MORD) at the Central level. The Civil Society institutions are also expected to be involved at all levels. In this chapter, the role of various state agencies such as Gram Panchayats, Block Development Officers (BDOs) / Programme Officers, Political Executives, Bureaucrats, NGOs and Political Parties have been examined in the implementation of MGNREGA.

Basic Implementing Agencies

MGNREGA envisages a collaborative partnership between the central government and the state governments. As per the Act, [MGNREGA Section 13(1)], the three tier Panchayati Raj Institution (PRI) is the principal authority for planning and implementing the scheme. The main implementation activities are performed at the village and the block level, while coordination activities are mainly at the block and district level.

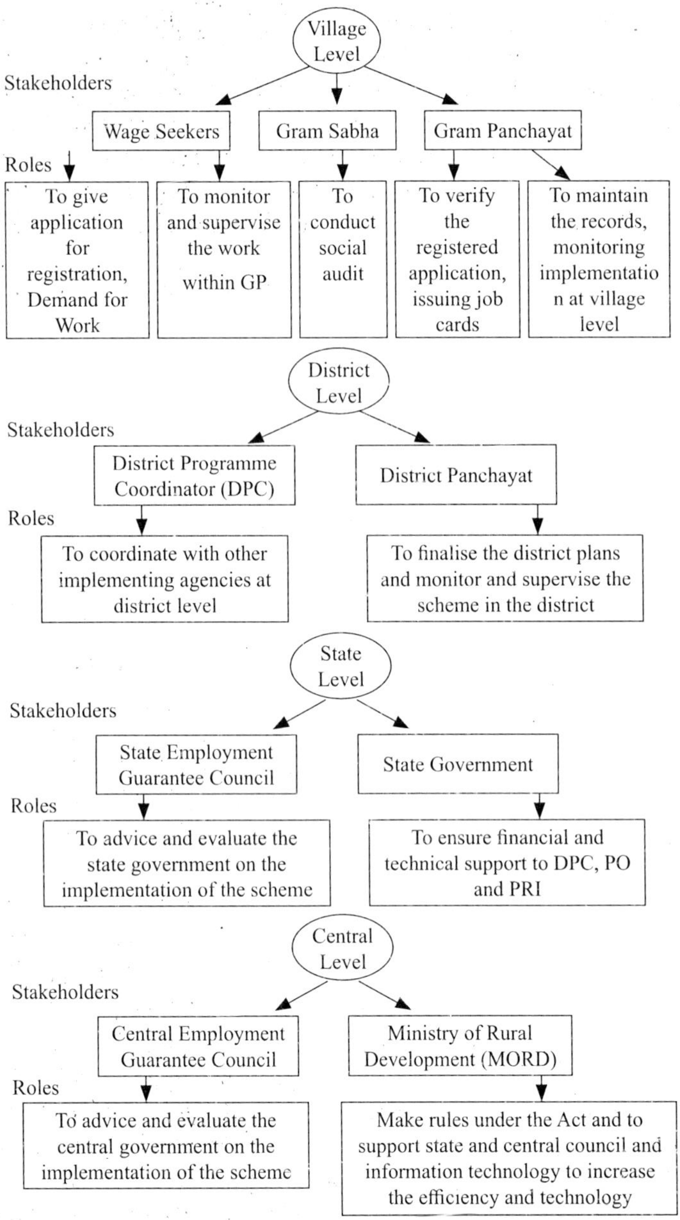

Fig. 5.1: State agencies and their roles in the implementation of MGNREGA as per the guidelines at different levels.

Gram Panchayat

Village Level
Gram Panchayat

- Recommend work to be taken up, monitor and supervise work conduct social audits of implementation, forum for sharing information, ensure transparency and accountability.
- Planning of work, registering households, issuing of job cards, allocating employment, executing 50 per cent of the work and monitoring implementation of the scheme at the village level.

Anchalik Panchayat

Block Level
Block Development Officer

- Planning at Block level, monitoring and supervision, executing work.
- To co-ordinate the work undertaken by Gram Panchayat and implementing agencies at block level.

Zila Parishad

District Level
DPC

- To finalise District Plans, monitor and supervise REGS in the District, execute work (other than Gram Panchayats work).
- Responsible for overall coordination and implementation of scheme at the District level

State Level

State Government

To formulate Rural Employment Guarantee Scheme (REGS) and Rules, designate State Rural Employment Guarantee Commissioner, to ensure timely release of State share, to ensure wide dissemination of information, to ensure administrative, financial and technical support to the implementing agencies.

SGEC

To advise State Government on implementation, monitoring and evaluation, decide on 'preferred work' under REGS, prepare annual reports.

State Level

MORD

Nodal Ministry for MGNREGA implementation, resource support to States, review, monitoring and evaluation of processes and outcomes and establish MIS.

CEGC

Advise GOI on MGNREGA related matters monitoring and evaluation and to prepare annual reports.

Fig. 5.2: Agencies and their roles in implementation of MGNREGA in Nalbari district of Assam.

As per the Act, the wage seekers are the primary stakeholders, because the Act is demand-driven and beneficiaries' exercise of rights as well as demand for work are the main principal key processes. According to the MGNREGA guidelines, the primary rights of wage seekers are to submit application for registration under the scheme. The wage seekers have the right to apply for a job card, demand for work, choice of work, right to work within 15 days of application, facilities of crèche, drinking water, first aid, etc. at the worksite as well as the right to get unemployment allowance in case the work is not provided within 15 days of submitting the application and receipt of wages within 15 days of work completion. In addition, active participation and involvement of the wage seeker is particularly important for ensuring efficiency, transparency and accountability.

Gram Panchayat is the local self-government at the village level. The chief (Gaonbuda) and the elected members of the Gram Panchayat are responsible for the implementation of the scheme at the village level. According to the MGNREGA guidelines (Section 13), GP is responsible for the planning of work as well as accountable for registering household, issuing of job cards, allocating employment, conducting social audit and maintaining Muster Roll (MR) of the implementation of the scheme at the village level. It is also expected to prepare a shelf of projects and annual plans.[1]

The Gram Sabha is the principal forum of the wage seekers to raise their voice and demand for employment. The Gram Sabha provides a platform to the wage seekers to obtain all relevant information from the state implementing agencies in relation to MGNREGA works. As per the Act, the Gram Panchayat is responsible for monitoring and supervising various works such as issuing of job cards, planning for work and registering household. It is the primary forum to conduct social audits for ensuring transparency and accountability for the implementation of the scheme.

As per the role of Gram Panchayat in the actual implementation of MGNREGA in Nalbari district was concerned, it was found that there was a wide gap between the intended roles of Gram Panchayat as mentioned in the programmes guidelines and the role being played by them on the field. The study showed that most of the members of Gram Panchayats (82.14 per cent) were not only ignorant about the basic objectives but also features and entitlements of the Act due to a low level of awareness. This lack of awareness was primarily due to the fact that they were not getting adequate training about the various provisions of the Act like its procedures and methods as well as obligations and rights. However, training was given to few respondents (30 per cent), which lasted for only a few days. With regard to social audit at GP level, about 66 per cent job card holders revealed that though social audit was conducted but it was not regular.

Further, as per the Act, the local vigilance and monitoring committee was set-up by Gram Panchayat with the local members of GP to monitor the progress and quality of work. In this regard, GP members did not have sufficient knowledge for this task. Therefore, the guidelines of MGNREGA provided an Employment Guarantee Assistants (Gram Rozgar Sahayak) in each panchayat. The study showed that only a few Gram Panchayats appointed Employment Guarantee Assistants to assist officials in executing MGNREGA works at GP level. Besides this, it was found that many Panchayats did not even have secretaries. As a result, the absence / irregularities of implementing officials led to improper implementation of the scheme at the village level. Further, it was revealed from the field study that the lack of technical support in selection and design of work at the GP level led to the inadequate implementation of the scheme in the district.

As per the Act, though the Gram Panchayat is expected to prepare the annual plan containing the facts and figures and accomplishments related to the implementation of the scheme. In Nalbari district, the study shows that 65 per cent of GP members said that annual plans and labour budget are presented by Gram Panchayat for approval of the Gram Sabha on 2nd October every year. After approved by the Gram Sabha, each Gram Panchayat submit its annual plan and labour budget along with a copy of the resolution of the Gram Sabha to the Programme Officer.

Further, the Bharat Nirman Rajiv Gandhi Sewa Kendra (BNRGSK) is constituted at the village level, to facilitate better co-ordination between Gram Panchayat and block level. However, it was found that in Nalbari district, the BNRGSK was hardly functional. The GP officials, too, did not have any knowledge that BNRGSK provided space for greater transparent interaction amongst the villagers for the efficient implementation of the scheme.Therefore, from the above data, it can be noted that the role of village authorities such as members of Gram Panchayat and other implementing officials at the village level in the implementation of MGNREGA was limited in Nalbari district due to absence of active participation among the officials and the lack of aptitude of GP to prepare an integrated holistic plan under the scheme. It was also observed from the field study that the elected representatives have limited information regarding their role and responsibilities in MGNREGA implementation.

Block Level

As per the Act, Intermediate Panchayat and Programme Officer are the implementing agencies at the block level. According to the MGNREGA guidelines, the Intermediate Panchayat is expected to approve the block level plan as well as planning, monitoring and supervising the works taken up by the Gram Panchayat. In Assam, the Intermediate Panchayat is known as Anchalik Panchayat which has rights to execute 50 per cent of total work at the block level.[2] In this regard, it was found that only one-third of the total work was executed by the Anchalik Panchayat at the block level in Nalbari district.

The Programme Officer, a full time dedicated employee, acts as a coordinator for MGNREGA. The primary responsibility of the Programme Officer is to ensure employment to the beneficiaries within 15 days of application. PO is also accountable for monitoring and supervision of work such as scrutinising village plans, matching employment opportunities with the demand for work, redressal of complaints and supervision of different implementing agencies to ensure that social audits are duly conducted by the Gram Panchayats.

Various other categories of supervisory staff such as engineers, data entry operators, accountants, etc. are also deployed at the block level to facilitate proper implementation of the programme. In addition, the Programme Officer is expected to set up the cluster level facilitation teams to provide a technical support to the Gram Panchayats. The PO is also responsible to assist the Intermediate Panchayat in carrying out the associated tasks at the block level in its implementation. In different blocks of Nalbari district, it was observed that there was no Programme Officer appointed for the purpose. At present, the Block Development Officers Act as the Programme Officer in all the seven blocks of Nalbari district and carry out the functions meant for PO. The Programme Officer scrutinises the Gram Panchayat's Annual Plans against the list of permissible works as specified in MGNREGA and collate all works within the Block and present the Block Plan before the Block Panchayat by 15th September. The PO has checked whether the wage material ratio for the list of works proposed for inclusion in the Annual Plan for the Gram Panchayat meets the requirements of the Act and schedule.

With regard to ensuring employment to the beneficiaries, there was undue delay in ensuring employment within 15 days of demand of work. About 58 per cent respondents revealed that they were not getting work within this time-frame. In this concern, study showed that on one hand, delay in the process of verification is caused at the GP level whereas on other hand non-availability of work causes inadequate work under MGNREGA.

As per the Act, BDO is responsible for ensuring that the unemployment allowances is paid to the job card holders, in case of employment not provided on time. It was found that in Nalbari district, unemployment allowances were not provided to the job card holders. Justifying this, BDOs' claimed that the job card holders were not aware and also the state government did not provide any funds for unemployment allowances. In addition, it was found that the BDOs' from all seven blocks of the district were not coordinating adequately to prepare shelf of projects.

District Level

The District Panchayat (Zila Parishad) and District Programme Coordinator are the implementing agencies at the district level. Zila Parishad is expected to finalise the Rural Employment Guarantee Scheme (REGS) and to monitor and supervise the REGS such as social audit, funds flow, payment of wages, progress and quality of works, qualitative aspects of implementation at district level. It was found that the process of work at the ZP level was very slow due to the lack of response of state government. Further, Zila Parishad apprises the state government about the budgetary requirements for the implementation of REGS. Once the funds are released by the state government, ZP was expected to utilise such funds to ensure employment to beneficiaries. However, the study showed that delay in process is caused both at the ZP level as well as at the state level causing delay in the implementation of the act. It also found that the labour budget was always expected to be prepared at the district level every year by December end for the approaching year under the Sub-section 6 of Section 14 of the MGNREGA, but it was mostly not sent within the required time-frame. It is mandated that labour budget is to be prepared in accordance with the process prescribed in Sections 13 to 16 of MGNREGA.

The state government designates a District Programme Coordinator, who can be either the Chief Executive Officer of the District Panchayat, or the District Collector, or any other District-level officer of appropriate rank. DPC is responsible for scrutinising the block plans, examination of the suitability and adequacy of works in terms of demand employment as well as their technical and financial feasibility. The DPC has to ensure strict adherence to the principles of bottom-up approach from planning to approval of the selected shelf of projects by each of the Gram Sabhas in the district. The other roles and functions of District Programme Coordinator are as follows:

Assist the District Panchayat in discharging its functions:

1. To accord timely, technical and administrative sanction to shelf of projects.
2. To release and utilise funds.
3. To ensure wage-seekers whether they are provided work as per their entitlements under this Act.
4. DPC is expected to review, monitor and supervise the performance of the Programme Officers and other implementing agencies in relation to MGNREGA works.
5. To develop annual plans for training and capacity-building of various stakeholders within the district.
6. Conduct periodic inspection of the works in progress and verification of muster rolls.
7. District Programme Coordinator shall keep the state government duly informed of progress of the implementation

of the programmes through the periodic reports and updates in the prescribed format.

8. Ensure that Rozgar Diwas is organised at every Gram Panchayat level at least once a month.
9. Ensure that social audits are done in all GPs once in six months and also make sure that follow-up action on social audit reports is taken.
10. To make sure that all transactions including issue of job cards, recording of applications for work, allocation of work, generation of wage slips and Fund Transfer Orders (FTOs), entries relating to work performed, delayed payment of wages, and unemployment allowance are made through officers of MGNREGA only.
11. Guarantee that all entries relating to works such as details of the shelf of works, GPS coordinates, status of implementation, photographs of works at three different stages are entered in MGNREGA at every required stage.

In Nalbari district, the Deputy Commissioner (DC) acts as a District Programme Coordinator and the Additional Deputy Commissioner-cum-Chief Executive Officer of the District Rural Development Agency (DRDA) is the Additional District Programme Coordinator (ADPC) under the scheme. The DC is responsible for overall coordination and successful implementation of the scheme, the ADCs assists the DC in carrying out the associated tasks in the district. The study showed that DC was conducting vigilance and monitoring at district level as well as ensured whether social audits are done by GP in six months. However, their involvement in terms of coordinating with other agencies like village level and block level was not satisfactory. For example, in scrutinising shelf of projects, estimates and budget, they were unable to do within the required time-frame due to lack of coordination with other agencies leading to delays in implementation of the Act.

At district level, officials are responsible for preparing District Prospective Plan (DPP) under MGNREGA to facilitate the vulnerable sections of the district. The DPP is a long-term, flexible, village-based plan, covering socio-economic aspects of development. DPP makes an informal analysis of poverty by ensuring the participation of the workers who are in need to work under the Act. Thus, DPP is an instrument to provide employment opportunities to the job card holders on the basis of their preference for the nature and time of work. DRDA is also considered to coordinate with other implementing agencies, financial institutions as well as technical institutions with a view to gather the support and resources required for the implementation, monitoring and evaluation of the DPP. In this respect, it was revealed that although plan for works was prepared yet it was not approved due to inadequate resources. It was also found that officials from DRDA were less concerned with the procedure for preparing the DPP and its implementation.

State Level

As per the Act, State Employment Guarantee Council is set up by state government under Section 12 of MGNREGA to advise the government and is made responsible for monitoring and evaluating the implementation of the scheme, however, it was found that they have largely failed to perform their responsibilities. The Government of Assam, P&RD Department vide notification dated March 21,2007, formulated "Assam Rural Employment Guarantee (State Council) Rules, 2006" and as per the provision, the council shall meet at least twice a year or more frequently as it may consider necessary to advise the state government on the implementation, evaluation and monitoring of the scheme. However, during the period of five years (2007-2012), it met only four times.

Further, SEGC is expected to prepare an annual report to be presented to the State Legislature. The SEGC decided the preferred works to be implemented and to recommend the proposals of works to be submitted to the central government by the state government under Schedule I Section 1 *(ix)* of the Act. It is expected to ensure all administrative, financial and technical support to the District Programme Coordinator, Programme Officer, PRIs and all other agencies involved in implementation. Further, the state government is to ensure training of officials regarding the various provisions of the MGNREGA. However, it was found from the various official records that they are unable to provide timely resource support including administrative, financial and technical to all implementing agencies involved in the process of imparting training.

The State Rural Employment Guarantee Commissioner (SREGC), appointed by the state government, is responsible to promote accountability and transparency as well as be responsive to the demands of workers. It is also expected to take necessary steps to improve the awareness regarding the scheme across the state. Besides this, the SREGC is the body to bring a system of flexibility in supervising quality of programme processes and expenditure.

As per the guidelines of MGNREGA, there was a provision of social audit[3] to be held every six months and for that the state government appointed social auditor but the time-frame was hardly ever followed. In this respect also, 57.14 per cent respondents revealed that no social audit was held in the required period, thus rendering social audit futile most of the time.

The state government is expected to design a financial management system to transfer and utilise funds. As per the Act, central government funds 75 per cent and the state government is expected to provide 25 per cent of total funds for the material cost of the schemes including payment of wages to skilled and semi-skilled workers, and unemployment allowances. However, it was found from the concerned state officials that the Government of Assam has ensured utilisation of only 20 per cent of total funds' towards the implementation of MGNREGA.

Central Level

As per the Act, the Government of India set up a Central Employment Guarantee Council for advising the central government related to MGNREGA works as well as monitoring and evaluating the implementation of the Act. It is responsible for preparing annual report to be laid before parliament on the implementation of MGNREGA. Further, the Ministry of Rural Development is expected for ensuring timely and adequate resource support to the State and Central Employment Guarantee Council. It is the duty of MORD to establish a Management Information System (MIS) and track data with the help of every critical aspect of the Information Technology (IT) to increase the efficiency and transparency of the processes as well as improves interface with the public. It also ensures that the implementation of MGNREGA at all levels is required to be made transparent and accountable to the public.

The Ministry of Rural Development is working as a nodal ministry at the central level to coordinate the working of MGNREGA at different levels, which are helpful in growing employment opportunities in rural areas. Regarding capacity-building, the Ministry of Rural Development recommended training and awareness programme to the implementing officials working at different levels such as state, district, block and village level. In Assam, National Institute of Rural Development & Panchayati Raj (NIRDPR-NERC) and State Institute of Panchayat & Rural Development (SIPRD) has organised such training programmes for the officials and elected representatives.

The Role of Non-Governmental Organisations (NGOs) and Political Parties in Implementation of MGNREGA

NGOs are supposed to play a significant role in poverty alleviation by assisting the poor in the rural areas. Most of the non-governmental organisations are working with government for the development of rural areas. It is said that NGOs are often able to reach segments of rural populations when the government programmes seems to be neglected or do not target the deprived sections of society. They often find their way into remote rural areas to identify the poorest segments of communities, deliberately seeking out those who are normally excluded from development processes because of their isolation, lack of assets and vulnerabilities.[4] The State Programme Coordinator is responsible for creating an enabling environment and a strong interface between the implementation machinery and the NGOs. Section 2(g) of MGNREGA states that

> "*implementing agency includes any department of the Central Government or a State Government, a Zila Parishad, Panchayat at intermediate level, Gram Panchayat or any local authority or Government undertaking or non-governmental organisation authorised by the Central Government or the State Government to undertake the implementation of any work taken up under a Scheme.*"

NGOs are expected to play an important role in generating awareness and mobilising the local people and also in ensuring transparency and accountability in monitoring and evaluating the scheme. Various studies reviewed that in States like Uttar Pradesh, Madhya Pradesh and Odisha, NGOs have played a significant role in terms of mobilising community, developing demand generation strategies, assistance of the GP in planning and measurement of work, maintenance of assets, facilitating to conduct social audit at GP level, wage payment, etc.

In Nalbari district, study shows that some efforts were made at the guiding beneficiaries in the process of formation of MGNREGA work at the local level for taking advantage of MGNREGA scheme through NGOs. It was observed that NGOs have provided the critical support to the PRIs for effective implementation of MGNREGA such as developing a thorough understanding of the baseline situation with respect to MGNREGA implementation such as capacity-building and exposure of local stakeholders and officials, PRI leadership and village communities, etc. Although, people's involvement in the planning process has been gradually increasing with the formation and strengthening of NGOs in villages, however, it still needs more involvement to enable the beneficiaries to access their rights and entitlements under MGNREGA.

Political parties are expected to play a pivotal role in the implementation of the MGNREGA such as spreading awareness, mobilizing workers and establishing workers' associations, etc. On the other hand, it was found that political parties were not very actively engaged in mobilising workers at the grass root level in the district except when they faced a challenge from other parties. About 71.42 per cent respondents revealed that there is a bias in work allotment according to party affiliation. Further, majority of respondents (56.42 per cent) said that politicians have ties with implementing officials during the process of releasing projects as well as funds. Further, they revealed that the members of political parties visit the villages' mostly during elections. They talk about deploying more resources under MGNREGA just before the elections. However, they fail to stay true to their commitment in the long run, thus severely affecting the effectiveness of the schemes. It has often been observed that communal tensions and strife between political parties disrupt the process of implementation of the scheme.

Evaluation of the Role of State Agencies in Implementation of MGNREGA in Nalbari District

The overall performance and the role of state agencies in the implementation of MGNREGA in Nalbari district are rather limited. It was observed from the field study that the state agencies have failed to fulfill the entrusted tasks due to lack of awareness among the implementing agencies about various provisions of MGNREGA, and lack of action from Zila Parishad and DRDA in terms of various activities of the programme. It is also evident that the officials from GP were aware about MGNREGA in nutshell, but not about the detailed provisions of the Act such as social audit, ombudsmen, etc.

Further, the block development officers of the district revealed that paucity of fund is one of the major hindrances in the implementation of MGNREGA. The state government never released money on time. On the other hand, the job card holders reported that members of Gram Panchayat were not giving proper information to them related to MGNREGA. The study showed that the involvement of middlemen was very common at each level of the implementation.

Thus, as far as the implementation of MGNREGA programme in Nalbari district is concerned, study shows that though the implementing agencies play an important role in planning and monitoring of the scheme, however, the poor participation of state agencies was leading to improper implementation of the scheme in the district. It was observed that various irregularities such as poor planning or choice of works not oriented towards the priorities envisaged under MGNREGA, inadequate shelf of works for execution throughout the year, lack of technical staff with GPs for planning, improper supervision, fake entries, limited capacity-building and awareness training has led to the limitations in the implementation of MGNREGA in Nalbari district. For effective implementation of MGNREGA schemes, there is need to have a co-operation between various implementing agencies, effective monitoring through conducting of social audit, and adequate trained human resources need to be deployed at the PRI level.

References

1. Operational Guidelines, The National Rural Employment Guarantee Act 2005, *op.cit.*, pp.4-5.

2. Bidtyut Mohonty, "Working of NREGA: Voices from Panchayats", Mainstream, Vol. XLVII, No. 15, 2009, p.5.
3. See NREGA, Section 17, Social audit, scrutinising all the records and works under the scheme are to be conducted regularly by the GP. It refers to an audit of all processes and procedures under the scheme, including registration of families, distribution of job cards, receipt of work, supervision of work, wage payments etc.
4. IFAD and NGOs: Dynamic Partnership to Fight Rural Poverty, Published by International Fund for Agricultural Development, *Working Paper*, 2000, pp. 09-10; https://www.ifad.org/documents.

6 Poverty Alleviation through MGNREGA

Economic planning has been generally perceived as one of the best strategies to achieve the goals of economic development as well as poverty alleviation. A number of poverty alleviation programmes have been implemented in the country over the past decades to improve the quality of life of rural poor by providing nutrition, health, housing, education, employment, information and broad casting and welfare of SCs/STs and OBC. Even after these poverty alleviation programmes a large portion of rural people still live below poverty line. There are also allegations that the fruits of poverty alleviation programmes, thus far, have been appropriated by the privileged few who have close proximity with political leaders as well as implementing officials.

A review of various poverty alleviation programmes indicated the need for a new comprehensive programme for the alleviation of poverty in rural areas. In addition, looking at the ineffectiveness of the top down approach of development, decentralised planning have been adopted to involve the local people in the process of development activities for which the programmes are undertaken. Several studies have indicated that the implementation of poverty alleviation programmes require an appropriate policy framework such as an effective delivery mechanism, adequate funds, people's participation at various stages of the formulation and implementation of the programmes like transparency in the operation of the schemes and adequate monitoring. In addition, greater functional and financial devolution to local government results in higher allocation of resources for social sectors and more efficient use of resources.[1]

Employment generation has been one of the major objectives for the development of planning in India, which is closely linked with poverty alleviation. The Tenth Five Year Plan (2002-07) specially focussed on poverty alleviation. In this context, MGNREGA was introduced during this period to improve the livelihoods of rural people when they suffer on account of absence of employment opportunities. It was meant to play a contributory role in transforming rural India by creating assets with the ultimate aim of poverty alleviation. MGNREGA is a right-based programme for rural poor especially for women to enable them to seek employment as per their choice and duration.

This chapter attempts to examine how MGNREGA was able to alleviate poverty in general and women in particular in Nalbari district. It examines the extent to which people have been benefitted from the various provisions of the Act such as getting job cards, work participation, worksite facilities, wage payments, gender relations in terms of equal wages for men and women, participation in decision-making process related to MGNREGA work, etc. The study also attempts to examine the implementation of the various provisions of the act. The data relating to this chapter was collected from respondents as identified in the methodology who were job card holders under the scheme in Nalbari district.

Socio-economic Background of Job Card Holders

To understand the impact of the various provisions of MGNREGA to the job card holders in Nalbari district, data have been collected to get information regarding their socio-economic background and their primary occupation before the implementation of the scheme as shown in Table 6.1.

Table 6.1: Socio-economic Background of Job Card Holders.

Sl. No.	Occupation	Male		Female	
		Number of respondents	Percentage	Number of respondents	Percentage
1.	Agriculture Labour	60	42.85	20	17.85
2.	Cultivator	30	21.42	28	20
3.	Skilled labour	16	11.42	20	14.28
4.	Unskilled labour	19	13.57	11	7.8
5.	Small Shop	9	6.42	7	5
6.	Domestic servant	6	4.28	9	6.42

Source: Field Survey.

Data shows that 42.85 per cent of the male respondents are agricultural labourers, 21.42 per cent are cultivators, 11.42 per cent are skilled labourers, 13.57 per cent are unskilled labourers and 6.42 per cent run small shops. Further, it is found that majority of women respondents i.e. 32.14 per cent are housewives, 20 per cent are cultivators, 14.28 per cent are skilled labourers, 7.8 per cent are unskilled labourers, 5 per cent run small shops and 6.42 per cent women respondents are domestic servants. From the field, it is found that majority job card holders working under the scheme belong to BPL families. Thus, it can be considered that MGNREGA provide them with a unique opportunity to earn additional income.

Approval of Job Cards

According to the MGNREGA guidelines, the basic identification of the beneficiaries for demanding employment is job card. The demand for employment in Gram Panchayat or at block level has to be made against the job card number. As per the Act, job card is to be issued within 15 days of registration after the verification of place of residence, age of members and the registered household. However, due to various irregularities with the implementing agencies, delays have been noted in the issuing of job cards as shown in Table 6.2.

Table 6.2: Days taken for Issuing Job Cards under MGNREGA in Nalbari District.

Sl. No	Days after submitting application to get Job Cards	Job Card Holders	
		Number	Percentage (%)
1	Within fifteen days	30	12.7
2	More than fifteen days	247	87.3
	Total	280	100

Source: Field Survey.

Data shows that only 12.7 per cent of job card holders received job card within the time frame while 87.3 per cent respondents did not receive job cards within 15 days. It was observed that there was undue delay in issuing of job cards after receipt of application as well as the practice of faulty allotment of job cards was very common in the study area. Further, the study showed that the implementing officials on the one hand, keep their job cards in the GP office and allot job to others in their name without their knowledge. The GP members on the other hand claimed that beneficiaries were not clear about the procedures of getting job cards and hence, it delayed issuing of job cards.

Participation in MGNREGA

Participation in MGNREGA is one of the pre-requisites to enforce the 'rights and entitlements' envisaged under the programme and make it a community-oriented and a demand-driven scheme. MGNREGA was introduced in Nalbari district during the FY 2006-07 and extended to all villages in the FY 2007-08. It is supposed to be 100 days of employment, guaranteed in every financial year to every household under MGNREGA. Although, official record showed a higher figure of number of days of employment provided under MGNREGA in Nalbari district, data shows that the average number of days of employment under this programme as per the household was rather low in the district.

Table 6.3: Year-wise number of days of Employment under MGNREGA in Nalbari District.

Sl. No.	No. of days worked	2007-2008	2008-2009	2009-2010	2010-2011	2011-2012	2012-2013
1.	1- 20 days	7	15	30	45	32	23
2.	21-40 days	6	12	39	40	28	18
3.	41-60 days	8	23	30	31	18	2
4.	61-80 days	5	11	20	25	16	12
5.	81-100days	2	4	8	23	16	23
6	Total	28	65	127	164	110	96
7.	Percentage of job card holders' participation (%)	10	23.21	45.35	58.57	39.28	34.28

Source: Field Survey.

It is evident from the table that only few respondents had got job opportunity under MGNREGA in the district. During the first year of the implementation of the scheme i.e. 2007-08, only 10 per cent respondents had got employment and in the FY 2008-09 and 2009-10, 23.21 per cent and 45.35 per cent respondents had got employment respectively. Further, in 2010-11, about 58.57 per cent respondents had got work and in 2011-12 and 2012-13, 39.28 per cent and 34.28 per cent respondents had respectively got work. Regarding 81-100 days of minimum employment, only 8.21 per cent respondents reported that they had got 100 days of employment during the FY 2010-11, only 5.71 per cent in 2011-12 and about 8.33 per cent respondents had got 100 days of employment in 2012-13.

Thus, as far as the norm of 100 days of employment under MGNREGA to every household in every financial year is concerned, it was found that for some, the job opportunity is only for a few days and some hardly got the norm as stated in the Act.

Further, with regard to regularity of employment availability under MGNREGA, about 71.42 per cent of total respondents revealed that employment was very irregular. It is evident from the Table 6.3 that the average number of days of employment availability under MGNREGA in Nalbari district was only 21-40 days per year due to which MGNREGA failed to generate adequate income opportunities in the district.

Worksite Facilities under MGNREGA

Worksite facility is a major concern for the better implementation of the employment guarantee act to enhance worker participation especially for women. Therefore, the study also examined whether job card holders are able to access worksite facilities under this programme when they worked. Data collected to answer this query is shown in Table 6.4.

Table 6.4: Worksite Facilities at the Worksites under MGNREGA in Nalbari District.

Sl. No	Worksite Facilities	Yes		No	
		Numbers of respondents	Percentage (%)	Numbers of respondents	Percentage (%)
1.	Drinking Water	49	17.5	231	82.5
2.	Shade for Rest	32	11.42	248	88.58
3.	Crèche for Children	--	--	280	--
4	Medicine	--	--	280	--

Source: Field Survey.

It is evident from the above data, though the Act provided worksite facilities to the job card holders for their convenience as well as for better quality work, however, only 17.5 per cent respondents had access to drinking water facilities and only11.42 per cent respondents said that shades for resting were available at the worksites. No other facilities such as first aid, crèche etc. were made available at the worksites. Although facilities like drinking water and shade for rest were made available at worksites, however, study shows that too was not universal. Women often complained that due to lack of crèche / child care facilities at worksite, they couldn't go for work. The lack of adequate worksite facilities appears to have discouraged participation under MGNREGA, particularly the lactating women, which affected average number of days of employment.

Payment of Wages

According to MGNREGA guidelines, every person working under the scheme is entitled to wages at the wage rate notified by the central government under Section 6(1) of the MGNREGA. Although, as per the Act, wage rates are fixed by the central government, however, under Section 6(2), the wages can be revised by the state government under Section 3 of the Minimum Wages Act, 1948. According to the FY 2013-14, the minimum wage rate per day under MGNREGA is 174, however, in Assam it is Rs.179. (See Table 6.5).

Table 6.5: Wage Rates under MGNREGA.

Sl. No.	Year	Minimum wages (Rs/per day)	Revised wages in Assam (Rs/ per day)
1.	2007-08	74	62
2.	2008-09	82	79
3.	2009-10	82	100
4.	2010-11	100	130
5.	2011-12	125	136
6.	2012-13	155	155
7.	2013-14	174	179

Source: nrega.nic.in.

Further, as per the Act, job card holders had to open accounts either in bank or in post-office. Although the system of biometric card payment of MGNREGA was introduced in 2013-14, however, it was hardly functional in Nalbari district due to deficit of computer equipment, electricity supply and internet connectivity. Therefore, beneficiaries collect their payment through bank or post-office accounts. In this respect, it is important to investigate whether job card holders have account in bank / post-office account in their name or not to get their wages. Data collected to answer this query is shown in Table 6.6.

Table 6.6: Beneficiaries Bank / Post-Office Account.

Sl. No	Account	Percentage (%)			
		Male		Female	
		Yes	No	Yes	No
1.	Post-office account	38.12	2	15.45	8
2.	Bank account	15	1.7	17.43	2.93

Source: Field Survey.

As against the guidelines, data shows from the selected sample that about 53.57 per cent respondents had account in post-office out of which only 15.45 per cent were female respondents and 32.43 per cent had bank account out of which 17.43 per cent were female respondents. As far as payment of wages within 14 days after completion of the work is concerned, it was found that only 7.5 per cent respondents received wages within this time period. Thus, the delay in payments of wages was a major problem for job card holders, particularly for women who were single earners of their families. Further, *benami* transactions were found in the rural areas of the district, due to which beneficiaries received less amount of wages/ payments than the Act provided. About 14 per cent respondents collected their payment through the name of GP members or through middle-men.

MGNREGA and Assets Creation

MGNREGA focusses on strengthening natural resource management and development through afforestation, drought proofing, flood control, water conservation, renovation of traditional water bodies, land development, etc. to reduce environmental degradation as well as development of infrastructure in the rural areas. Independent studies like the one conducted by Indian Institution of Science, Bangalore, have indicated that the implementation of MGNREGA generate multiple environmental benefits leading to improved water availability, soil fertility and increased crop production. MGNREGA works contributed to improving the adaptive capacity of rural people in several States like Rajasthan, Madhya Pradesh, Andhra Pradesh, Karnataka and Sikkim. Although, it was observed that in Nalbari district, MGNREGA has not shown much positive result. About 53.57 per cent of respondents stated that however some developments in the area of agriculture and local level natural resources management such as water conservation and water harvesting, renovation of traditional water bodies, flood control, provision of irrigation facilities, rural connectivity roads, plantation, etc. had benefited not only the job card holders but also benefitted the entire village. Regarding the quality of MGNREGA assets and their maintenance, about 38 per cent of them stated that the quality of assets was very poor in areas like construction of road land development etc. as it was claimed that the roads constructed under the scheme need to be repaired after every season.

Table 6.7: Level of Awareness of the Major Provisions of MGNREGA.

Sl. No.	Provisions of MGNREGA	Numbers of respondents	Percentage of respondents (%)
1.	Hundred days of employment	130	46.42
2.	Application for employment	45	16
3.	Knowledge about minimum wages	120	42.85
4.	Equal wages for men and women	124	44.28
5.	Time limit to getting work	28	10
6.	Time limit to getting wages	32	11.42
7.	Extra wages for travel long	183	65. 35
8.	worksite facilities	102	36.42
9.	Medical assistance for injured at the worksite	29	10.35
10.	Social audit	25	8.92
11.	33 per cent employment opportunities for women	20	7.14
12	Unemployment allowances	7	2.5

Source: Field Survey.

From the above, it can be noted that there has been an improvement in the rural society in terms of poverty alleviation like fulfilling basic human needs of the rural people as well as livelihood security by ensuring employment opportunities and asset creation through MGNREGA, but very slowly. It is noted that the poor level of awareness amongst beneficiaries compounded the problem. In this respect, it is important to know the level of awareness among the job card holders about various provisions of MGNREGA in the district. Data collected from the workers regarding their awareness about MGNREGA provisions and entitlements is shown in Table 6.7.

Data shows that only 16 per cent of respondents knew that application had to be submitted for getting employment, 10 per cent respondents were aware of the time limit for getting work and only 11.42 per cent were aware of receiving wages within 14 days of completion of work. As such, they were not able to claim unemployment allowances. With regard to minimum days of guaranteed employment and minimum wages, only 46.42 per cent and 42.85 per cent respectively were aware of this provision. It was found that only 7.14 per cent respondents knew that 33 per cent employment opportunities should be given to women. Further, interestingly, although knowledge about the basic entitlements of the Act was found to be rather low, however, awareness about extra wages to be paid for work undertaken in distant areas was quite high (65.35 per cent).[2] In addition, there was a wide difference between the male (66.78 per cent) and female (33.22 per cent) respondents with regard to their level of awareness about the Act across the district. Thus, the lack of awareness and worksite facilities, delay in issuing of job cards and payments of wages, irregularities in work, etc. are the major obstacles in the proper implementation of the scheme.

Gender Equity and MGNREGA

In a gendered society, there is inequality between men and women in their status and positions, which has resulted in an inferior ranking of women vis-à-vis their male counterparts. Gender is a social and cultural construct. Gender differences lead to variations in social positions, roles and behaviour, attitudes and personalities of men and women in a society. The unequal distribution of income and control over resources (including property, assets and financial capital) between women and men, women's lack of decision-making power, the unequal distribution of household tasks, gender-based violence, and the constraints imposed on women's socio-economic mobility due to legal, cultural and labour market barriers, all Act as contributory factors which cause and compound women's poverty. In all societies, both men and women work, but perform different tasks and with differential impact and outcomes. Further, the difference in work between men and women are shaped by two kinds of economic divisions between production and reproduction and between organized or formal economics and unorganised or informal economics. These divisions are constituted by gender which has an impact on women's empowerment. The gendered distribution of assets and the resultant fallout on women substantially limits empowerment in a patriarchal society.

In this context, MGNREGA has been envisaged as gender sensitive scheme by providing employment opportunity to women. There are various provisions under the scheme which aims to ensure that women have equitable and easy access to work, decent work conditions, equal payment of wages and representation on decision-making bodies. It has provided mobility to women at village level which is one of the essential factors of empowerment. Various studies across the country conducted by independent researchers have shown that women have indeed benefited from MGNREGA in many ways i.e. women have participated on a large scale and received equal wages with men and earned incomes of their own in most of the districts of India.

In Nalbari district, both men and women work under MGNREGA, however, men get more preference than women. As the society is patriarchal in nature in which women are generally dominated by men in terms of production activities, decision-making process, etc. In this regard, the study examined whether women respondents were facilitated in various activities of MGNREGA.

Table 6.8: Women Respondents facilitated in Various Activities.

Sl. No.	Factors	Numbers of respondents	Percentage of respondents (%)
1.	Registration of job cards	57	40.71
2.	Providing information about work	27	19.28
3.	Work opportunity	15	10.71
4.	Providing wages as per prescribed Norms	55	39.28
5.	Solving problems of women at Worksite	20	14.28
6.	Women voice in the selection of Work	4	2.85

Source: Field Survey.

According to the data collected from the field, it was seen that only 40.71 per cent women respondents had got support from the officials regarding job card registration and only 19.28 per cent respondents had got information about MGNREGA work through the villagers and panchayat. It was noted that there is a general perception that women are too weak to do manual work, they should not work outside the home along with male workers. Majority of women beneficiaries had failed to receive any support from family members to join MGNREGA work. Study shows that from the women respondents, only 10.71 per cent got the opportunity to work with in the village and hardly any women were allowed to go to distant places for earning higher wages. Further, about 73.57 per cent women respondents revealed that GP members/middle-men instead of providing work to them allotted it to others in their name. Work availability for women was, therefore, marginal and also highly irregular.

This means majority of women participants did not get opportunity to work under MGNREGA. Thus, women's economic security, productivity and their empowerment gets limited. It is evident that because of the patriarchal norms and values, women are still not getting space under the scheme. As a result, women were denied the chance of becoming beneficiaries under MGNREGA programme due to the opposition of family members. As a result, the patriarchal norms prevent women's access to employment and thereby, men get preference over work than women.

Women's Work Participation under MGNREGA

Work participation under the scheme is reflected in exercising their rights because MGNREGA is a right-based programme. Scheduled II of the Act emphasises on the word "priority" should be given to women in the allocation of work in such way that "*at least one-third beneficiaries should be women*". Although the Act assured to provide 33 per cent of total employment to women beneficiaries, however, in the study area employment could not reach the prescribed norms. (Table 6.9).

Table 6.9: Workforce of Women Beneficiaries under MGNREGA in Nalbari District.

Sl. No	Year	Numbers of respondents	Percentage of work participation (%)
1.	2007-08	4	2.85
2.	2008-09	10	7.14
3.	2009-10	21	15
4.	2010-11	27	19.28
5.	2011-12	16	11.42
6.	2012-13	13	9.28

Source: Field Survey.

Data shows from the field survey that only 2.85 per cent women beneficiaries had got work during the FY 2007-08 and in 2008-09 and 2009-10, 7.14 per cent and 15 per cent women beneficiaries had respectively got work. In addition, only 19.28 per cent women beneficiaries had got employment in 2010-11 and in the FY 2011-12 and 2012-13, 11.42 per cent and 9.28 per cent women beneficiaries had respectively got employment. Thus, one of the objectives given in the guidelines i.e. at least one-third beneficiaries should be women did not materialise.

Receiving Wages: Opening of individual post-office / bank account by women beneficiaries is one of the gender-sensitive initiatives taken up in MGNREGA. Although majority of the women respondents have opened post-office / bank account yet only 49.28 per cent women respondents stated that payment was made as per prescribed work norms,[3] and 3.57 per cent women respondent stated that they earned some limited income through MGNREGA. Further, some others were not getting equal wages due to influence of middle-men.

Generating Income: Although MGNREGA encouraged women respondents to generate income through employment opportunities however, majority of women respondents were not getting adequate employment opportunities under the scheme in Nalbari district. It was found from the field study that only 5 per cent women respondents said that earning from MGNREGA facilitated their children's school enrollment. About 88.57 per cent respondents revealed that MGNREGA has brought limited progress in their daily life in terms of food consumption, health care and nutrition. As a result, it can be seen that women beneficiaries' contribution to household income through MGNREGA is negligible and they are unable to overcome poverty.

Thus, the study shows that women are still confined to the domain of the household and various restrictions are encountered by them even with in the domain. Further, it was found that women have limited opportunities to raise their voice in the public sphere as well as within households. Moreover, the patriarchal structure within the economic sphere and in wage labour excluded women from the MGNREGA work. The degree of inequality between men and women in terms of wages, allocation of works, access to worksite facilities and women voices has affected gender relations.

Participation of Women in the Gram Sabha meetings and its Impact:

The Gram Sabha is the platform where the beneficiaries and the members of GP directly interact with each other and also discuss issues relating to MGNREGA activities, accounts of expenditure in the respective areas. MGNREGA aimed at enabling women's participation in decision-making process in terms of participation in GP meetings, selection of works, social audit process as well as planning and monitoring of MGNREGA works at GP level. Participation at the GP level through the programme is a way to influence the power relations at household level and was also expected to bring sustainable change in gender relations.

Table 6.10: Women Participation in Gram Sabha.

Sl. No.	Participation of women beneficiaries in Gram Sabha	Numbers of respondents	Percentage (%)
1.	Regularly	17	12.14
2.	Intermittently	26	18.57

Source: Field Survey.

Data collected from the field shows that although women are now getting opportunities to participate in Gram Sabha meetings in the rural areas of the district, the decision-making process is still under male domination. About 12.14 per cent women respondents attend Gram Sabha regularly, 18.57 percent women respondents attend only intermittently. The reasons why majority of women were not attending meetings is because their families prevented them, while some of them were overburdened by domestic work and some were discouraged from attending the meetings and they were generally not allowed to voice their opinion. As a result, women got limited access to information as well as decision-making process in the household and community level.

With regard to selection of work, women respondents (28.57 per cent) of those who attend Gram Sabha meetings revealed that they didn't get preference for selecting work under MGNREGA. As such, male counterparts prevented them in choosing work in the worksite causing inconvenience to women. Athough the programme guidelines suggested that the involvement of women in social audit process is an important component to promote community level involvement, however, in Nalbari district, participation of women in the social audit process as well as planning and monitoring was negligible. Their involvement in the management of assets was rather limited. As a result, it led to limited achievement of benefits, to gain access to resources in the household as well as at the community level. This has affected gender relations in the social, economic and political sphere that substantially limited empowerment of women.

Thus, from the study we found that the contribution of MGNREGA to alleviate poverty was rather limited. Although, the various provisions of this programme meant to alleviate poverty by providing employment opportunites to rural poor, however, it has hardly benefited the beneficiaries in overcoming poverty in the district. The potential of the scheme has not been fully realized due to acute shortage of functionaries, absence of strong grievance redressal system, weak financial institutions and monitoring system, lack of accountability, corruption, etc. In addition, lack of effective people's participation as well as lack of awareness failed to ensure employment opportunities to the beneficiaries.

References

1. K.R. Gupta, *Poverty in India*, New Delhi: Atlantic Publishers, 2008, p.200; S.L. Goel, *Rural Health Education*, New Delhi: Deep & Deep Publication, 2008, p.134.
2. Under MGNREGA extra wage to be paid if work was given beyond 5 kilometers from the Gram Panchayat, Operational Guidelines, The National Rural Employment Guarantee Act, 2005, p.27.
3. Every person working under MGNREGA shall be entitled to wages at the minimum wage rate fixed by the state government (or the competent authority concerned) for agricultural labourers under the Minimum Wages Act, 1948, unless the wages have been notified by the central government under Section 6(1) of the Act. Equal wages shall be paid to both men and women workers under the provisions of the Equal Remuneration Act, 1976, Operational Guidelines, *The National Rural Employment Guarantee Act, 2005*, p.26.

7 A Way Forward

The culture of poverty, inherited from the colonial times, has been India's bane. It has perpetuated India's slow growth, low productivity, stunted populace and decline in India's standing in the World. India is deficient and behind several neighbouring countries' in HDI markers and has barely attempted to approximate the MDGs agreed at the UN. However, poverty alleviation remained a major goal of India's development strategy since independence. Many programmes for poverty alleviation like IRDP, Antodaya, etc. have been undertaken by the Government of India.

India lives in its 600,000 villages. Rural poverty is endemic and all pervasive. Many factors contribute to this malaise but the major one is lack of employment opportunities, except during the cultivation season. In order to directly attack the problem of unemployment, MGNREGA was introduced as an effective means for alleviating poverty.

The research work examined the efficacy of MGNREGA on the anvil of the Nalbari district in Assam. It examined the role of oversight agencies, political articulators of opinion, media, district administration implementing agencies, NGOs associated with MGNREGA, etc., in effective implementation of the scheme in the district.

MGNREGA continues to be the largest poverty alleviation and wage employment programme for rural India. The main focus of this programme is to enhance livelihood security by generating employment, providing income earning opportunities by creating rural assets and targeting vulnerable sections of the society including institutions in planning of the creation of assets and localising the UN endorsed Sustainable Development Goals (SDGs) such as poverty alleviation, gender equity, reduce distress migration, etc. which builds local government institutions to ensure sustainable development.

Some of the positive outcomes of MGNREGA noticed are that the agricultural labourers got work opportunity in the lean agricultural season. It has helped to reduce rural emigration to urban areas by providing work opportunity within the village. Further, the labour wage increased in the district because of higher wages offered by MGNREGA. It has influenced the rural poor to work under MGNREGA. Local distress was alleviated.

MGNREGA has also reduced wage discrimination in labour market. It was found that MGNREGA played a significant role in improving the rural economy by giving equal wages to rural people, especially for women. It became a tool of empowerment for the rural women through wage employment. According to the women beneficiaries, MGNREGA made changes in their economic and social status in the district. It was observed that women beneficiaries got an opportunity to open their own post-office / bank account through the programme and took decisions to spend money according to their needs. Further, MGNREGA has also helped to convert unpaid work into paid employment.

MGNREGA has given opportunity to the vulnerable sections such as SCs, STs, landless, women headed households, etc. to participate in the planning and decision-making process at the Panchayat level. MGNREGA has made direct impact to improve the conditions of rural poor in the Nalbari district through creating rural infrastructure such as afforestation, water conservation, renovation of traditional water bodies, micro-irrigation, land development, road connectivity, etc. These positive features of MGNREGA help to fulfill the basic human needs of the rural poor and ensure their empowerment and inclusion in the national development endeavour. However, various shortcomings were discovered in the field in the process of implementation of the scheme that hindered to achieve to targets set for the district.

The successful implementation of MGNREGA programme depends on an appropriate policy frame-work, availability of adequate funds and sustained delivery mechanisms. As per the MGNREGA Act, the implementing agencies such as Gram Panchayat, BDO's,

District Rural Development Agency and NGOs were tasked to ensure efficient implementation. However, it was found that there was a wide gap between stated guidelines and practice at the grassroots level. This came about because of paucity of funds, lack of human resources, limited knowledge about the programme amongst the state agencies, lack of training programmes for implementing agencies and absence of coordinated involvement of different agencies. Shortage of staff increased the work load on the officials which led to poor implementation of the programme. In addition, technical departments of the government were also unable to provide adequate support to the implementing officials.

Further, irregularities at the GP level in maintaining muster roll such as incomplete list of workers / beneficiaries, improper implementation, misinformation on the women's reserved quota, (i.e. one-third reservation), data recorded in incomprehensible manner, bogus statement of expenditure, etc. were also observed. In addition, the involvement of GP members appears to be limited to merely identifying beneficiaries. The study found that lack of capacity of GPs to prepare perspective plans on rural infrastructure led to poor implementation.

As per the MGNREGA Act, the social audit is organised village-wise through Civil Society Organisations (CSOs), political representative as well as NGOs. It includes verification of the muster rolls, costs of work, payment of wages, worksite facilities, etc., in order to ensure transparency, accountability, vigilance and awareness at the grassroots level. However, the study found that the reports of social audit were neither prepared in prescribed format nor were they submitted on time. It was also found that the records of social audit were not available in a systematic manner.

As per the Act, ombudsmen should be appointed in every district (under Section 27) for greater transparency. However, it was claimed that the state government was unable to appoint ombudsmen under MGNREGA. The grievance redressal system was very weak in the district. Most of the job card holders were unaware of their rights to complain against concerned authorities. Further, the study found that the village level vigilance monitoring committees were inactive and non-participating.

Getting job cards, allocation of work, timely payment of wages and worksite facilities were not as per the approved programme guidelines, mostly due to delay in release of funds from state as well as central government, delay in submission of audit reports and utilisation certificates to the central government. It was claimed that the central government could not release funds on time due to incomplete process of collecting social audit reports from the state. Further, it was found that workers were unable to get work even when funds were available due to delays in sanctioning of schemes. As a result, the major objectives of the scheme i.e. generating income by ensuring employment opportunities and asset creation to overcome poverty was rather limited in the district.

Ensuring gender equity through MGNREGA, which is a fundamental feature of the programme, was also limited. The study shows that women were getting limited opportunity in various activities at the ground level such as choice of work, timing and location, participation in the process of social audit, Gram Sabha meetings, etc. Although the Act aims at providing work opportunity to women, however, the study revealed that in Nalbari district of Assam, women failed to get adequate work opportunity due to irregularities, limited information, prevalence of patriarchy and social differentiation regarding work, both in the public sphere and within the household. It was also found that caste and religion limited the participation of women. Women from certain castes and religions are forbidden from working outside home, particularly in agricultural and manual work. Women from upper castes have not historically worked on other people's land and thus tend to decline MGNREGA work even when they were physically capable of participating and were in need of the income, while the women from lower castes agreed to work outside home. Similarly, Muslim women who practice the Purdah system refrain from appearing in public, limiting their ability to participate. In 2009-10 and 2010-11, 3.28 per cent and 4.12 per cent upper caste women worked under MGNREGA respectively. These challenges considerably reduced the empowering capacity and wage employment opportunities for women.

For the effective participation of rural people under MGNREGA, adequate knowledge of the programme is required, especially amongst those who are working under the scheme. However, the study shows that in the rural areas of the district, due to lack of awareness amongst the beneficiaries, non-availability of work, lack of work-site facilities, delay in payments of wages, etc., MGNREGA failed to reach the prescribed targets in the district.

The study found that the development of rural infrastructure such as construction of approachable and motorable road, water conservation, etc. took place but again only on a limited scale. Further, the guidelines of the Act prohibited the use of machines at the worksite. However, the study shows that most of the work was completed by using machines and the expenditure was made against the job card holders' payments. As a result, beneficiaries got less employment opportunity under MGNREGA.

Most of the local officials had close linkages with political leaders and bureaucrats which resulted incorrupt practices in implementation such as issuing of false job cards, payments of wages through *benami* transactions, not respecting the gender quota, showing unnecessary expenditure, etc. As a result, the basic entitlement of the scheme i.e. ensuring livelihood security by providing employment opportunities to the rural poor as well as a degree of social protection to the vulnerable sections of the society i.e. women was seen to be limited in the district.

MGNREGA has various shortcomings in implementation because of weak monitoring system, communication problem, lack of coordination between different departments, nepotism, political influence, etc. In addition, caste, religion, patriarchy, lack of transparency and corruption in issuing job cards, inadequate social audit added to the less than optimal effectiveness of MGNREGA in Nalbari district. Assistance to the poor by providing employment opportunities in terms of fulfilling basic needs such as food, clothing and health facilities fell fairly short of target.

The scheme can be more effectively implemented if the following is taken care of:

1. Sensitised approach should be followed for beneficiaries. Members of Gram Panchayat should make beneficiaries aware of the provisions of the scheme for enhancing transparency. Self-help Groups (SHGs) of women should be in the central place for all aspects of MGNREGA-right from

sensitisation of people about the potential of getting work, getting job cards, planning for work, and more importantly, organising the works. Community–based monitoring and social audit is required which could be done through women collectives and the people's groups.

2. Gram Panchayats should maintain all crucial control documents such as application registers, employment registers, muster roll-stock / issue / receipt registers, complaint registers, etc. mandatorily to ensure transparency and assessment of the scheme and for redressal of grievances. Mobilisation of people to participate in Gram Sabha should be ensured to plan and decide MGNREGA works and procedures to achieve the targets.
3. Efforts towards ensuring convergence of MGNREGA for sustainable livelihood to the targeted rural community and localising SDGs, the Sectoral Departments need to take steps to organise awareness generation programme and perspective building to allow beneficiaries to get maximum benefits. The capacity-building training for elected representatives of panchayats can also help to spread awareness amongst elected representatives to achieve the sustainable development through the scheme.
4. Decentralised planning and intensive people's participation at the micro-level need to be facilitated. Participation of large sections of society in the planning process would give a new dimension among MGNREGA work-seekers of their entitlements. Periodical training methods in capacity-building have to be imparted to encourage their positive participation. Further, it is necessary to develop a methodology for carrying out state-wise evaluation studies through third party appraisals for assessment of the impact of MGNREGA on individual households, labour market, migration cycle and efficacy of the assets created.

Conclusion

Rural masses depend mostly on agriculture and farming which suffers from either constant or decreasing returns. This has perpetuated poverty. Lack of diversification results in worsening the employment and poverty in the country remains major challenges for the policy-makers. MGNREGA was designed to make a forceful dent on these challenges. Although many shortcomings were found in the implementation of MGNREGA, there is conclusive evidence that it has provided employment opportunity and created durable assets in the study area. The success of the scheme, to a great extent, depends on the initiatives taken by the Gram Panchayats in the preparation of Action Plans and in their execution. Members of Gram Panchayats are trained to take up various activities permitted under the MGNREGA and help in implementation in an integrated manner.

In the future executive, members of GP need to be trained to efficiently formulate proposals and projects. The need is to be sufficiently empowered. The National Institute of Rural Development and Panchayati Raj, MoRD, GoI has initiated massive capacity-building programme to sensitise the officials from sectoral departments, elected members of PRIs and mobilising the rural local people to achieve the sustainable livelihoods through the programme. This could be thoroughly disseminated throughout the country for effectively tackling the rural poverty.

Bibliography

Primary Sources

Government Reports:

Directorate of Economic and Statistics, *Economic Survey of Assam, 2011*, Government of Assam, 2011.

Directorate of Economics and Statistics, *Economic Survey*, 2004-05, New Delhi: Government of India, 2005.

Government of Assam, *Assam Human Development Report 2003*, Planning and Department, Guwahati, 2013.

Government of Assam, *Economic Survey of Assam, 2012-13*, Directorate of Economic and Statistics, Planning and Development Department, 2013.

Government of Assam, *Economic Survey of Assam, 2011-12,* Directorate of Economic and Statistics, Planning and Development Department, 2012.

Government of India, *Annual Report 2000-01*, Ministry of Rural Development, New Delhi, 2001.

Government of India, *Annual Report 2005-06,* Ministry of Rural Development, New Delhi, 2006.

Government of India, *Annual Report of 2010-11*, Planning Commission of India, 2011.

Government of India, *Economic Survey of India, 2012-2011*, Director of Economics and Statistic, 2011.

Government of India, *Ministry of Information and Broadcasting, India 2011*, New Delhi: Publication Division, 2011, p.799

Government of India, *Operational Guidelines: The National Rural Employment Guarantee Act 2005*, Ministry of Rural Development, New Delhi, 2006.

Government of India, *Press Note on Poverty Estimates 2009-10*, Planning Commission of India, 2012.

Government of India, *Report of Progress of Land Reform*, Part I and IV, Planning Commission, New Delhi, 1963.

Government of India, *The National Rural Employment Guarantee Act 2005, Operational Guidelines,* Ministry of Rural Development, New Delhi, 2005.

Ministry of Law and Justice (Government of India) India, 2005, *The National Rural Employment Guarantee Act*, Publication Division, New Delhi, 2005.

Ministry of Rural Development (Government of India) India, 2011, Department of Rural Development: *The Mahatma Gandhi National Rural Employment Guarantee Act*, New Delhi, 2011.

The Chronic Poverty Research Center, *The Chronic Poverty Report 2004-05*, Published by Manchester: UK, 2005.

United Nations, Report of the World Summit for Social Development 2005, 2005.

World Bank, World Development Report 2000-2001, New York, Oxford University Press, 2001.

Secondary Sources

A. Books:

Ahmed, Joyeeta, *Poverty Alleviation in Assam*, New Delhi: Hope India Publications, 2011.

Ahuja, Ram, *Social Problems in India,* New Delhi: Rawat Publications, 2004.

Aray, Sadhna and Anupam Roy (eds.) *Poverty, Gender and Migration*, New Delhi: Sage Publications, 2006.

Aziz, A., *Poverty Alleviation in India*, New Delhi: Ashish Publishing House, 2001.

Balakrishna, S. and S.V. Rangacharyulu, *Poverty Decline and Human Development Factors in Some States*, Hyderabad: NIRDPR, 1999.

Bandyopadhyay, K. R., *Poverty Alleviation and Pro-Poor Growth in India*, New Delhi: Asian Institute of Transport Development, 2007.

Basu, Rumki, *Economic Liberalization and Poverty Alleviation: Social Sector Expenditures and Centre State Relations*, New Delhi: Deep & Deep Publications, 2000.

Behra, M.C. (ed.), *Globalization and Development Dilemma: Reflections from North-East India*, New Delhi: Mittal Publications, 2004.

Beneria, L. and Feldman, S. (eds.), *Unequal burden: Economic Crises, Persistent Poverty and Women's Work,* Boulder: Co: West View Press, 1992.

Bhuryan, Arun Chandra, *Political History of Assam*, Guwahati: Government of Assam Publications, 1998.

Bhatt, M. S., *Poverty and Food Security in India: Problems and Policies*, Delhi: Aakar Books Publications, 2004.

Brara, J.S., *The Political Economy of Rural Development: Strategies for Poverty Alleviation*, New Delhi: Allied Publishers, 1983.

Chadha, G.K. and Sharma, Alakh, *Growth, Employment and Poverty: Change and Continuity in Rural India*, Delhi: Vikas Publishing House, 1997.

Chambers, Robert, *Rural Development, Putting the Last First*, London: Longman Publications, 1983.

Chaudhari, P., *The Indian Economy: Poverty and Development*, New Delhi: Vikas Publishing House Pvt. Ltd, 1992.

Chelliah, Raja. J. and Sudarshan, R., *Income, Poverty and Beyond*, New Delhi: Social Science Press, 2001.

Dandekar, V.M. and Rath, Nilakantha, *Poverty in India*, Pune: Indian School of Political Economy, 1971.

Deb, K., *Rural Development in India since Independence*, New Delhi: Sterling Publishers, 1986.

Dreze, J. and Sen, A., *India: Economic Development and Socia lOpportunity*, Vol. I to III, Oxford: Claredon Press, 1995.

Dreze, J. and Sen, A., *Indian Development: Selected Regional Perspectives*, Oxford: Clare Land Press, 1997.

Dreze, J. and Sen, A., *The Political Economy of Hunger*, Vol. I to III, Oxford: Claredon Press,1990.

Franda, Marcus, *India's Rural Development: An Assessment of Alternatives*, London: Indiana University Press, 1974.

Friedmen, John, *Empowerment: The Politics of Alternative Development*, Cambridge: Wiley-Blackwell, 1992.

Gaur, Keshav Dev., *Poverty Alleviation and Rural Diversification*, New Delhi: Sunrise Publications, 2007.

Galbraith, J.K., *The Nature of Mass Poverty*, New Delhi: Penguin books, 1984.

Griffith, Geoff, *Poverty Alleviation for Rural Women: Indian Voluntary Organisation and Village Development*, Avebury: Aldershot Hants, 1994.

Gupta, K.R., *Rural Development in India,* Vol. 2, New Delhi: Atlantic Publishers, 2003.

Hebel, J., Samadi and Nurrochmat, D. (eds.), *Poverty Alleviation: Concepts and Experiences, focussed on Indonesian Case*, Gottingen: Cuvillier Verlag, 2004.

Hooja, R. and Parnami, K.K., *Development Administration and Rural Development,* Jaipur: Aalekh Publishers, 2007.

Jayal, N.G., *Democracy and the State: Welfare, Secular and Development in Contemporary India*, New Delhi: Oxford University Press, 1999.

Jain S.P. and Polman, Wim, *A Handbook for Trainers on Participatory Local Development: The Panchayati Raj Model in India*, Bangkok: RAP Publications, 2003.

John, F., Deshingkar, P., Johnson, C., and Start, D., *Policy Windows and Livelihood Futures: Prospects for Poverty Reduction in Rural India,* New Delhi: Oxford University Press, 2006.

Khan, M. Adil., *Economic Development, Poverty Alleviation and Governance: The Asian Experience*, New Delhi: Ashgate Publishing Limited, 1996.

Khera, Reetika (ed.), *The Battle for Empowerment Guarantee*, New Delhi: Oxford University Press, 2011.

Kohli, A., *Democracy and Development in India*, New Delhi: Oxford University Press, 2009.

Kohli, A., *The State and Poverty in India: The Politics of Reform*, Cambridge: Cambridge University Press,1987.

Krishna, M., *Poverty Alleviation and Rural Poor*, New Delhi: Mittal Publications, 2003.

Krishnaraj, Maithreyi, *Gender, Food Security and Rural Livelihoods,* Kolkata: Stree Publications, 2007.

Kornmesser, Allen, Changing Indian Agriculture: Agrarian Society, Economic, Planning and Development Since 1947 in LaRue, C. Steven (ed.), *The India Handbook*, London: Rutledge Publications, 1997.

Kumar, Anand, *Nation Building in India: Culture, Power and Society,* New Delhi: Radiant Publications, 1999.

Kumar, Anand, *State and Society in India*, New Delhi: Radiant Publications, 1989.

Lewis, Oscar, *Five Families: Mexican Case Studies in the Culture of Poverty,* New York: Basic Books, 1959.

Mali, D.D., *Economic Problems and Planning in Assam*, New Delhi: Omsons Publications, 1993-94.

Maheshwari, S.R., *Rural Development in India: A Public Policy Approach,* New Delhi: Sage Publications, 1995.

Mathur, Kuldeep, "Designing Poverty Alleviation Programmes: International Agencies and Indian Politics" (ed.), *Development Policy and Administration*, New Delhi: Sage Publications, 1996.

Mehta, Asha Kapoor, Sourabh Ghosh, Deepa Chatterjee and Nikhila Menon (eds.), *Chronic Poverty in India*, New Delhi: Indian Institute of Public Administration, 2003.

Mehta, S.R., *Poverty, Population and Sustainable Development*, New Delhi: Rawat Publications, 1997.

Mehta, S.R., *Rural Development Policies and Programmes: A Sociological Perspective,* New Delhi: Sage Publications, 1984.

Mishra, Baidyanath, *Poverty, Unemployment and Rural Development*, New Delhi: Ashish Publishing House, 1991.

Mishra, Naveen, *Poverty in South Asia*, New Delhi: Authors Press, 2001. Misra, B.N., *Poverty, Unemployment and Rural Development*, New Delhi: Ashish Publishing House, 1991.

Misra, Baidyanath and Rajkishor Meher, *Economic Liberalisation and Regional Disparities in India*, New Delhi: A.P.H. Publishing Corporation, 2000.

Misra, S. N., *Poverty Alleviation Programmes and Gram Panchayats*, New Delhi: Mittal Publications, 1997.

Ministry of Rural Development, Government of India, *MGNREGA Sameeksha, An Anthropology of Research Studies on the Mahatma Gandhi National Rural Employment Guarantee Act, 2005, 2006–2012*, edited and compiled by Mihir Shah, Neelakshi Mann and Varad Pande, New Delhi: Orient Black Swan,2012.

Ministry of Rural Development, Government of India, *MGNREGA Sameeksha - II, An Anthropology of Research Studies on the Mahatma Gandhi National Rural Employment Guarantee Act, 2005, 2012-14*, New Delhi: UNDP, 2015.

Moynihan, D. P. (ed.), *On Understanding Poverty*, New York: Basic Books, 1968.

Murty, RanjaniK. and Lakshmi Sankaran*, Denial and Distress: Gender, Poverty and Human Rights in Asia*, Bangalore: Book for Change, 1999.

Murty, T. S., *Assam the Difficult Year*, New Delhi: Himalaya Books, 1997. Myrdal, Gunnar, *The Challenges of World Poverty,* New York: Penguin International Edition, 1970.

Narasaiah, M. L. and Raju, G. J., *Rural Development and Anti-Poverty Programme,* New Delhi: Discovery Publishing House, 1999.

Oyen, Else, Miller, S.M., and Sayed Abdus Samad, *Poverty a Global Review,*

Handbook on International Poverty Research, New Delhi: Rawat Publications, 2003.

Prabhu, Seeta K. and Sudarshan, R., *Reforming India's Social Sector: Poverty Nutrition, Health and Education*, New Delhi: Social Science Press, 2002.

Rao, C.H. and Hans, L., *Economic Reform and Poverty Alleviation in India*, New Delhi: Sage Publications, 1996.

Radhakrishna, R. and Shovan Ray, *Handbook of Poverty in India: Perspectives, Policies, and Programmes,* New Delhi: Oxford University Press, 2005.

Radharkrishna, R. and Subbarao, K. (eds.), *India's Public Distribution System: A National and International Perspective*, Vol. 380, Washington: World Bank Publications, 1997.

Sainath, P., *Everybody Loves a Good Drought: Stories from Indian Poorest Districts*, New Delhi: Penguin Books, 1996.

Sen, Amartya, *Poverty and Famines: An Essay on Entitlement and Deprivation*, New Delhi: Oxford University Press, 1981.

Sengupta, Keya, *Genesis of Human Development in North-East India*, New Delhi: Concept Publishing Company, 2009.

Shah, S.M., *Rural Development Planning and Reforms*, New Delhi: Abhinav Publications, 1997.

Sharma, J.K., *Rural Development in South Asia,* New Delhi: Authors' Press, 2001.

Singh, B.D., *Planning for Rural Development and Poverty Alleviation,* New Delhi: Mittal Publications,1992.

Singh, M., *Rural Development, Administration and Anti-poverty Programmes*, New Delhi: Deep and Deep Publishers, 1988.

Singh, R.K., *Poverty and Sustainable Development: Third World Perspectives,* Vol. I. New Delhi: Abhijeet Publications, 2005.

Sinha, R.K., *Understanding Poverty*, New Delhi: Anamika Publishers, 2003.

Srinivasan, T.N. and P.K. Bradhan, *Rural Poverty in South Asia*, New Delhi:Oxford University Press, 1988.

Thakur, Dalip, S., *Poverty, Inequality and Unemployment in Rural India*, New Delhi: B.E. Publishing Corporation, 1985.

Thakur, R., Rural *Development and Planning in India*, New Delhi: Deep and Deep Publishers, 1989.

Tiwari, Nupur (ed.), *MGNREGA and Gender Equity*, New Delhi: Kanishka Publishers, 2015.

Vaidyanathan, A., *India's Economic Reform and Development,* New Delhi: Academic Foundation, 2003.

Articles:

Aiyar, Y. and Samji, S., "Improving the Effectiveness of National Rural Employment Guarantee Act", *Economic and Political Weekly*, January 2006, pp. 320-326.

Alam, Barkat, "Poverty Alleviation, Welfare, Economic Development and NGOs – Some Observations", *Indian Journal of Public Administration*, Vol. 45, No. 1, January-March, 1999, pp.34-50.

Bagchee, Sandecp, "Poverty Alleviation Programmes in Seventh Plan—An Appraisal", *Economic and Political Weekly*, Vol. XXII, No. 4, January 24, 1987.

Bhalla, Sheila, "Trends in Poverty, Wages and Employment in India", *Indian Journal of Labour Economics*, Vol.40, No.2, April-June 1997, pp. 215-222.

Bhatia, B. and Dreze, J., "Employment Guarantee in Jharkhand: Ground Realities", *Economic and Political Weekly*, July 2006, pp. 3198-3202

Bhattacharyya, Rituparna and Vauquline, Polly, "A Mirage or a Rural Life Line?, Analysing the impact of Mahatma Gandhi Rural Employment Guarantee Act on Women Beneficiaries of Assam", *Space and Culture*, Vol.1, No.1, 2013.

Bigman and Srinivasan, "Geographical Targeting of Poverty Alleviation Programs: Methodology and Applications in Rural India", *Journal of Policy Modeling*, Vol. 24, 2002.

Carter Michael R. and Christopher B. Barrett, "The Economics of Poverty Traps and Persistent Poverty: An Asset-Based Approach", *The Journal of Rural Development Studies*, Vol.42, No.2, 2006, pp. 178-199.

Chakraborty, P.,"Implementation of Employment Guarantee: A Preliminary Appraisal", *Economic and Political Weekly,* February, 2007, pp. 548-51.

Dalal, R.S., "Poverty Alleviation - What IRDP Did?," *The Indian Journal of Political Science,* Vol. LXII, No.2, April-June 2006, pp.311-322.

Das, V. and Pradhan, P., "Illusions of Change", *Economic and Political Weekly*, August 2007, pp.3283-87.

Dash, Satya Prakash, "State Administration: Development, Finance and Crime", *The Indian Journal of Political Science*, Vol. LXV, No.3, July-September 2004, pp. 435-456.

Datt, G. and Ravallion, M., "Why have some Indian States Done Better than Others at Reducing Rural Poverty?", *Economica*, 1998.

Dev, Mahendra S., "Economic Reforms, Poverty, Income Distribution and

Employment", *Economic and Political Weekly*, Vol.35, No.10, March 2000, pp. 823-835.

Dhanpat, "Poverty in India: Dimensions and Causes", *Third Concept*, March 1997, pp. 47-50.

Dollar, Devid, Robert Gatti, "Gender Inequality, Income and Growth: Are Good Times Good for Women", Policy Research on Gender and Development, The World Bank, Development Research Group, Poverty Reduction and Economic Management Network, Research Working Paper Series, No,1,1999.

Dreeze, Jean, "Poverty in India and the IRDP Delusion", *Economic and Political Weekly*, Vol. 26, No. 29, September 1990.

Dubey, A., "Hunger and poverty in North-Eastern States, Implications for Food Security", paper presented at the National Seminar on Food Security in India, CESS Hyderabad, March 2000.

Fukuda-Parr, S., "What does Feminization on of Poverty Mean? It isn't Just Lack of Income", *Feminist Economics*, 1999.

Gaiha, Raghav, "Poverty, Development and Participation in India", *Asian Survey*, Vol.35, No.9, September 1995, pp. 867-878.

Gaiha, Raghav, "On the Targeting and Cost- Effectiveness of Anti-Poverty Programmes in Rural India", *Development and Change*, Vol.32, No.3, March 2001, pp. 309-42.

Hasim, S.R., "Dimensions of Poverty and Approach to Poverty Alleviation", *IASSI Quarterly*, Vol. 13, No.1, 1996, pp.55-67.

Hirway, Indira, "Garibi Hatao: Can IRDP Do it?", *Economic and Political Weekly*, Vol.20, No.13, March 1985, pp. 561-564.

Holmes, Rebecca, Nidhi Sadana and Saswatee Rath, "An Opportunity for Change? Gender Analysis of the Mahatma Gandhi National Rural Employment Guarantee Act," Working Paper, No 53, Overseas Development Institution, 2011.

Hussain, Tassadduk A., "Assam fails to deliver NREGA Promises: Survey", *The Hindustan Times*, New Delhi, April 2010.

Jacob, A. and Varghese, R., "National Rural Employment Guarantee Act Implementation-I: Reasonable Beginning in Plakkad, Kerala", *Economic and Political Weekly*, December, 2006, pp. 4943-45.

Jha,R., Gaiha, R., Pandey, M. K., and Kaicker, N, "Food Subsidy, Income Transfer and the Poor: A Comparative Analysis of the Public Distribution System in India's States", *Journal of Policy Modeling*, Vol. 35, No. 6, 2013, pp. 887-908.

Khera, Reetika, "Trends in Diversion of PDS Grain", *Economic and Political Weekly*, Vol. 46, No.21, 2011, pp.106-114.

Kelkar, Govind, "At the Threshold of Economic Empowerment: Women, Work and Gender Regimes in Asia", ILO Asia-Pacific Working Paper Series, 2013.

Khera, Reetika and Nayak, Nandini, "Women Workers and Perceptions of the National Rural Employment Guarantee Act in India", Paper Presented at the FAO-IFAD-ILO Workshop on Gaps, Trends and Current Research in Gender Dimensions of Agricultural and Rural Employment: Differentiated Pathways out of Poverty, Rome, 2009.

Krishnamurty, J., "Employment Guarantee and Crisis Response", *Economic and Political Weekly*, March 2006, pp. 789-790.

Krishnan, Gopal, "India: The 100 Poorest Districts, 2001", *Man & Development*, Vol.-XXXVIII No.1, March 2006, pp.169-174.

Kumar, Vijay S., "Mahatma Gandhi National Rural Employment Guarantee Act – A review", *Kurukshetra*, Vol.59 No.3, January 2011, pp. 10-14.

Liu Yanyan, and Christopher B. Barrett, "Heterogeneous Pro-Poor Targeting in India's Mahatma Gandhi National Rural Employment Guarantee Scheme", *IFPRI Discussion Paper*, International Food Policy Research Institute,2012.

Moghadam, V. M., "The Feminization of Poverty and Women's Human Rights", *Social and Human Sciences*, 2005.

Mohonty, Bidtyut, "Working of NREGA: Voices from Panchayats", *Mainstream*, Vol. XLVII, No. 15, March 28, 2009.

Murgai, R. and Ravallion, M., "Employment Guarantee in Rural India: What Would it Cost and How Much would it Reduce Poverty?" *Economic and Political Weekly*, July 2005, pp. 3450-3455.

Nidheesh, K.B., "National Rural Employment Guarantee Programmes & Amelioration of Poverty among Tribal People", *Indian Journal for Social Development*, Vol.8, No.2, December 2008, pp.229-244.

Pathe, V. P., "Poverty Eradication: A New Paradigm", *Yojana*, Vol.42, No.8, August 1998, pp. 87-90.

Panth, Ananth S., Social Network and Food Security in Rural Karnataka, *Economic Political Weekly*, Vol.32, No. 12, April 1997, pp. 756-758.

Pattnaik, Bikram, K., "Poverty, Population and Rural Social Development", *Kurukshetra*, Vol. 46, No.11, August 1998, pp. 3-8.

Pattanaik. B. K, "National Rural Employment Guarantee Scheme: Some Preliminary finds from Hosiarpur Distrct", *Kurukshetra*, Vol.57, No.6, April 2009, pp. 35-38.

Pearce, Diana, "The Feminization on of Poverty: Women, Work, and Welfare," *Urban and Social Change Review*, 1978.

Pradhan, Rudra P., "An Economic Approach between Human Development and Poverty in North-East Region India" *Information Management and Business Review*, Vol. 2, No. 1, January 2011, pp. 26-37

Pankaj, Ashok, Rukmini Tankha, "Empowerment effects of the NREGS on Women Workers: A Study in Four States", *Economic & Political Weekly*, Vol. XLV, No.30, July 2010, pp.45-49

Ray, Amul, "Delivery Systems for Rural Development in India: A Field View of Institutional Linkage", *Public Administration and Development*, Vol. 5, No. 4, October-December 1985, pp. 362-367.

Rath, Nilakantha, "Garibi Hatao: Can IRDP DoIt?", *Economic and Political Weekly*, Vol. 20, No. 6, February 1985.

Ravi, Shamika and Monika Engler, "Workfare as an Effective Way to Fight Poverty: A Case of India's NREGS", *World Development*, 2013.

Sen, Amartya, "Editorial: Human Capital and Human Capabilities", *World Development*, Vol. 25, No. 2, 1997, pp. 1959-1961.

Shah, Mihir, "National Rural Employment Guarantee Act: A Historic Opportunity", *Economic and Political Weekly*, December 2004, pp. 5287-5291.

Sharma, Amita, "Right Based Legal Guarantee as Development Policy: The Mahatma Gandhi National Rural Employment Guarantee Act", India: *UNDP*, 2010.

Sharma, Jogender, "Potential and Challenges", *Kurukshetra*, Vol.58, No.2, December 2009, pp. 3-7.

Sikligar, P.C., "Impact Assessment of Wage Employment (MGNREGS): A Study in Tripura", *Indian Journal of Public Administration*, Vol. LVIII, No.1, January-March 2012, pp. 91-95.

Sanyal, Subhashree, "Millennium Development Goal: Why So Far", *Yojana*, Vol. 55, December 2011, pp.54-56.

Shariff, Abusaleh, "Assessment of Outreach and Benefits of National Rural Employment Guarantee Scheme of India", the *Indian Journal of Labour Economics*, Vol.52, No.2, 2009, pp. 243-248.

Suna, Birendra, Sanjay Pratap and Anand Kumar, "*Responding to People's Protests about Poverty:* Making and Implementation of the National Rural Employment Guarantee Act in India", Paper Presented at the International Conference at Manchester University, 2010.

Vadyanathan, A., "Poverty and Development Policy", *Economic and Political Weekly*, Vol.36, No.21, May 2001, pp. 1807-1822.

Venugopal, K.R., "The Reluctant Guarantee", *Social Change*, Vol. 37, No.1, March 2007, pp.1-6.

United Nations 1995, "The Copenhagen Declaration and Programme of Action: World Summit for Social Development", New York: United Nations Department of Publications, 1995.